The Prodigy by Honoré Daumier

To Edward Weiss

Acknowledgements
Many friends, colleagues and pupils have contributed directly or indirectly to the creation of this book. My particular thanks go to Gerald Wragg for the insight he gave me into Alexander's teaching and philosophy, to John Ogdon for the support which he has expressed in his Foreword, and not least to Ronald Stevenson, who has helped so much in so many ways, including the loan of photographs.

The Pianist's Talent

Harold Taylor

Foreword by John Ogdon

A new approach to piano playing
based on the principles of
F Matthias Alexander and Raymond Thiberge

Kahn & Averill, London

First published by Kahn & Averill in 1979
First paperback edition published in 1982
This revised and enlarged edition published in 1994 by
Kahn & Averill
9 Harrington Road, London SW7 3ES
Copyright © 1979 & 1994 by Harold Taylor

The photograph of F Matthias Alexander on page 108
is published courtesy of The Society of Teachers of the
Alexander Technique: © S.T.A.T. 1993

British Library Cataloguing in Publication Data
A catalogue record for this book is available from the British Library

ISBN 1 871082 52 8

Printed in Great Britain by
Halstan & Co Ltd., Amersham, Bucks.

Contents

List of Illustrations

Foreword

"I am the vessel through which *Le Sacre* passed".

Stravinsky's famous words describe a composer's mental condition at a certain time, and the mental condition of a creator is parallelled by the muscular condition of a performer.

I think many performers have the feeling, if a performance is going well, that the music is playing itself and that they are the agents through which the music passes.

Harold Taylor has convincingly shown, through his study of the work of Raymond Thiberge and F. Matthias Alexander, that this feeling is the result of being in a certain state of muscular co-ordination.

This co-ordination may be unconscious; the playing of a pianist at the elementary stage has been observed to improve, temporarily but markedly, under hypnosis. And the analytical hypnosis of Dr. Dahl must have had a marked effect on Rachmaninoff's co-ordination.

There can be no doubt, however, that this co-ordination of muscle and mind can be approached consciously, and Harold Taylor's application of the methods of Raymond Thiberge should play an important part in bringing the conscious attainment of a beneficial muscular co-ordination within the grasp of students of any age.

John Ogdon

Preface

During the past decade there has been a welcome upsurge of interest in the work of the late F. Matthias Alexander, especially amongst those who practise the performing arts. When Alexander died in 1955, his teachings were hardly known, although he had lived and taught in Britain for nearly fifty years, founded his own training school in 1930 and published four books which have made a major contribution towards understanding the workings of that mysterious mind-body entity which we call the 'self'. Nowadays, the teaching of 'Alexander Technique' — his unique method of co-ordinating mind and body — is a growth industry. Apart from its adoption by several leading music and drama colleges, more and more people from every walk of life are discovering its benefits and a great impulse has been given by the paper-back publication of Dr. Wilfred Barlow's brilliantly lucid treatise: *The Alexander Principle* (Arrow Books, London 1975). My reference to Alexander on the title page of this book should therefore have some significance for some readers.

On the other hand, the name of Raymond Thiberge is unlikely to mean anything. No account of his work has been available in English and since his death in 1968 he remains as shadowy a figure in his native

France as Alexander was in Britain. Also, like Alexander, Thiberge was a lone pioneer — in his case, in the fields of both musical and general education — who founded his own institute in 1932 and published three important books before the Second World War, long before the climate of opinion was amenable to their acceptance.

There are other parallels between Thiberge and Alexander. Both found their wider vocations by accident, arising from decisive experiences which occured when they were seeking solutions to problems connected with their earlier careers as piano teacher and elocutionist respectively. In both cases, finding the help of established 'authorities' inadequate, they solved their problems by using their own resources of feeling, imagination and reason.

Most important, the conclusions reached by Professor Thiberge about pianistic performance are almost identical with those reached by Alexander as to how people 'perform' in general, allowing for certain differences of terminology and approach. It is ironic that neither knew of the other's existence, since so much in each man's work confirms the findings of the other.

The behaviourist psychologists define learning as "the modification of behaviour patterns through experience". At my first impromptu encounter with Raymond Thiberge, he modified my own pattern of behaviour with regard to playing the piano within the space of a few minutes and the result was a dramatic improvement in all aspects of my performance. After that experience, I naturally had to return to him for lessons, if only to convince myself that I had not been under some kind of hypnosis — even though Professor Thiberge did not possess that essential attribute of most hypnotists: eyesight. However I soon learned that his extraordinary teaching method was based on no more than a series of easily verifiable facts and that paradoxically,

his very blindness had been the instrument of their
perception.

I also realised that Thiberge's teaching had important
implications with regard to that mysterious inborn
capacity for achievement which we call 'talent'. Talent
is fundamental. Without it we can do little; blessed
with a sufficiency, we can conquer the world. Yet most
writers tend to ignore it, because it appears to be
beyond discussion, like the colour of one's hair or the
shape of one's nose — and even less capable of modification. Admittedly, it is one of the riddles of the
universe which no geneticist has so far solved and we
know that no amount of training, surgery or psychiatry
can create it where it does not already exist. But thanks
to Alexander and Thiberge, it is now at least possible
to make some valid statements as to how it works
for us; furthermore, to describe how we ourselves
ought to work in order to ensure that this most precious
asset is neither dissipated nor devalued, but on the
contrary, is invested to yield increasing dividends.

The scheme of this book is as follows:—
1. An enquiry into the nature of talent and what may
   be learnt from it concerning the most desirable
   conditions for playing the piano.
2. The means of fostering these conditions, showing
   how the teaching of F. Matthias Alexander in the
   general sphere of human behaviour is linked to the
   teaching of Raymond Thiberge in the particular
   sphere of piano playing.
3. Some conclusions which may be drawn with regard
   to practising, repertoire and related topics.

Although there are many quotations from Thiberge
and Alexander throughout the text, I must emphasise
that this book is essentially a personal document,

presented for the greater part in my own terms. In particular, I confess personal responsibility for the concept of expanding versus contracting postural conditions on which its central argument hinges and also for the deductions which relate piano playing to the art of dancing. To describe in words those things which in reality can only be experienced is no easy task. How far I have succeeded, the reader must judge from his own experiences, which I hope, and believe, can only become increasingly beneficial as a result of studying the following pages. The translations from the works of Professor Thiberge are mine; the remarks of certain eminent pianists which lack context references are remembered from conversations which I have been privileged to enjoy on various occasions.

Preface to the Second Edition

For this edition, I have added two chapters: *Freedom and Flexibility* and *The Thumb*. They should be studied in conjunction with *The Teaching of Raymond Thiberge*, which they complement and amplify. The bibliography has also been revised but otherwise the book remains substantially unaltered; experience continues to confirm its validity.

Finally, I must thank Peter Feuchtwanger for permission to quote him in Chapter 9 and for his support generally.

Mark Hambourg aged 9

1 Towards a Definition of Talent

All the great musicians of past and present have this much in common: they displayed their gifts early in childhood. It was said of Handel that he could sing before he could talk and one thinks immediately of Mozart, classic example of the 'Wunderkind'. Mozart's feats as a child prodigy have entered history, but his case is not exceptional. Beethoven was an equally remarkable child. In our own time, faced with the pianistic achievements of the octogenarian Arthur Rubenstein, it is hard to remember that he too was once a child prodigy. It is easier to remember that Mark Hambourg was an infant prodigy, because he remained an 'enfant terrible' at the piano throughout his life. But the most extraordinary case of this century, or possibly any other century, is that of Erwin Nyiregyhazi, the great Hungarian pianist who died recently in California, who was a prolific composer by the age of four and played the Beethoven *C minor Concerto* when he was five.

The most important point about infant prodigies is that their talent manifests itself spontaneously, untaught and unlearned. In fact, it is often the discovery of talent in the child which has prompted its parents into arranging for it to be trained, not the reverse. Even in professional households such as those of Mozart and Beethoven, where musical studies would begin early as a matter of course, the parents have been surprised by their offspring 'jumping the gun'. Artur Schnabel tells the following story: "When I was six years old, my elder sister . . . started to take piano lessons. My mother told me . . . that I, without having lessons, succeeded in doing what she was taught much quicker than she. *I simply went to the piano and did it*" * (My italics).

Talent may be briefly defined as the ability to perform without training, the amount of talent displayed being in inverse proportion to the amount of training required. It would be wrong to assume from the above story that Schnabel's sister was without any talent for the piano, just because her brother's talent shone so obviously. There is no demarcation line between 'no — talent' and 'talent'; there are only varying degrees of talent, just as in harmony, regarded from a purely acoustical standpoint, there are no concords and discords but only various degrees of dissonance. The most untalented person can usually perform a five-finger exercise without training; at the other end of the scale, we find the 'super-talents' such as John Ogdon, whom I remember sight-reading the Brahms *D minor Concerto* at the age of nine.

The previous sentence does Mr. Ogdon less than justice, for what arrested my attention on the top corridor of the old Royal Manchester College of Music was not a sight-reading as we normally understand the term. It was a *performance*, with all the technical and musical accomplishment that the word implies, which I discovered to my astonishment was taking place at sight. Like Schnabel, he 'simply went and did it', but in his case the dimensions are larger. In

* Schnabel, A. *My Life and Music*, pp. 7-8 (Longmans Green and Co. 1961)

the words of Professor Thiberge: "Talent is a matter of degree, virtuosity a matter of scale". At all levels, there is a correlation between the degree of talent and the amount of virtuosity, both mental and physical, which is available to the individual on demand, without having to be worked for. The integration of thought and action which the virtuoso takes for granted as part of his equipment is seldom achieved by lesser talents, even after long years of study and practice.

All practising aspires to the condition of talent; we practise in order that we may need not practise. Louis Kentner has a splendid aphorism: "There is no such thing as a 'difficult' piece. A piece is either impossible — or it is easy. The process whereby it migrates from one category to the other is known as practising".* To which we can add the rider that the speed of migration is determined by the amount of talent at one's disposal. Mr. Kentner himself learned Brahms's *First Piano Concerto* in three days. It might take another performer three weeks; another three months. Furthermore, the quality of execution displayed in the finished product by the slow learner is not likely to surpass that of his quicker colleague. Undoubtedly, practice and experience can go a long way towards compensating for lack of spontaneous ability, but on the common ground of maturity where trained and talented eventually meet, the instinctive ease of the latter is still recognisable. In the Biblical parable, it will be remembered that the servant who was endowed with five talents was able to increase his quotient to ten; he who possessed only two, although he was also able to double his quotient, was still not able to achieve the amount which the more fortunate servant originally possessed — which sums up the whole question of

* Kentner, L. *Piano* p. 90   (Kahn and Averill 1991)

training versus talent. The infant prodigy remains a prodigy.

Fortunately for us lesser mortals the gap between the 'haves' and the 'have-nots' in the world of talent is not permanently fixed at a certain distance and can be narrowed, as I hope to show. There is no fixed quota of talent which is automatically at the disposal of the individual during his or her lifetime. Experience, training, environment, in fact all aspects of existence contribute to the manifestation or the inhibition of one's potentialities. There are many former infant prodigies who are just 'also rans' today, even some who have disappeared into oblivion by the age of twenty. Then there are the occasional feelings of being 'off form' experienced by even the most talented performers, when they fall below their customary standard of efficiency. It is important to realise that if these performers were consistently 'off form', then the superiority of their talent would not be recognised — for the simple reason that it would not exist. Conversely, the 'ordinary' pianist sometimes finds himself playing better than usual or is able to sight-read beyond his normal capacity. In a nutshell: as we *are*, so we perform.

A student once asked me: "What has Horowitz got that I haven't?". The short answer to this question is: "Nothing!" Neither Horowitz, nor any other virtuoso, possesses any extra fingers or muscles, specially designed limbs or nervous system. The superiority of the virtuoso stems not from the possession of any extraordinary capacities, but solely from the way in which his capacities function.

It is interesting to note the great strides made in piano playing during the past hundred years. Moritz Rosenthal, one of Liszt's greatest pupils, remarked in 1924 that many of his contemporaries could play as well as Liszt, if not better. (Rosenthal went on to say that if Liszt were alive, he would immediately recognise the fact — and then would immediately set out to place himself at the top again.) As early as 1912, Busoni suggested that a kind of 'musical Darwinism' might be at work, comparing the proliferation of virtuosity with the capacity of the children of simple peasants to deal expertly with problems of electrical wiring which would baffle their parents.

The super-talent of today may well become the accepted norm of tomorrow. Liszt's *B minor Sonata* is now almost an obligatory debut piece and even works like *Islamey* or the *Don Giovanni Fantasy* are no longer the exclusive property of a limited number of pianistic giants, as they were fifty years ago. It may well be that the pianistic animal has become more adapted to the demands made upon it. At the same time, modern methods of teaching are generally less destructive to the growth of talent than they were in the nineteenth century. Whatever the reason, the proliferation of virtuosity supports my original point that the highly talented pianist is neither a biological 'sport' nor the possessor of extra-human capacities, but merely an optimum example of the way in which these capacities operate when applied to piano playing.

Here is another point which cannot be too strongly emphasised: the way in which Horowitz functions is just as normal to him as the way in which you or I function is normal to us. He would find it highly abnormal, if not impossible, to use himself as badly as certain 'blacksmiths' of the profession one hears occasionally, who are incapable of making a single sound in the same way as the great masters, because their pattern of behaviour prevents them from doing so in the first place. George Antheil, in his scurrilous autobiography, *Bad Boy of Music*, describes the 'black-

smith' approach in lurid terms: "The sweat — great
slithering streams of it — pours down you . . . . This
next round with the Steinway would be a lot more
comfortable in fighting trunks" . . . . and so on.[3]
He assumes from his own experience that this is the
normal lot of any concert pianist, but real mastery
of the keyboard is delineated by the very absence of
this kind of struggle. Fine piano playing results from
fine co-ordination, a particular interaction of brain,
body and keyboard which intrinsically precludes any
mis-directed effort. Under ideal conditions, far from
having to strive for his results, the pianist literally
enjoys the co-operation of his instrument to the extent
that it feels as if it is playing itself. The greater his
talent, the more readily he approaches this ideal, simply
because the necessary conditions of co-ordination are
already present in himself.

Talent may therefore be expressed as *capacity for
co-ordination*. It is this that the prodigy instinctively
relies upon to provide his means of performance without training and guides him to success as a mature
virtuoso. It is my contention that to increase one's
capacity for co-ordination, however slightly, is in-
finitely more rewarding than any amount of hard
labour at the keyboard which does not serve that
purpose. In fact, the continuous application of mis-
directed effort can actually cause a reduction in the
amount of talent at one's disposal, as we shall see.

Furthermore, it is impossible to perform above or
below the level of co-ordination which exists at any
given moment, as any artist who has had the frustrating
experience of being 'off form' will testify. He knows
that he can play better, but his prevailing condition
of co-ordination at the time will not allow him to do

---

* Antheil, G. *Bad Boy of Music*, pp. 3-4 (Doubleday, N.Y. 1945)

so. Yet it is fortunate that these fluctuations exist, because they offer rays of hope for the lesser-talented and at the same time provide a starting-point for my examination, in the following chapter, of the mechanism of co-ordination.

Anton Rubinstein aged 12

2 The Basis of Co-ordination

Every student of the piano will be able to recall those occasions when, apparently by chance, a sudden improvement has been experienced in the performance. Mysteriously, the gap between thought and action has narrowed, and everything has gone well. If only we could play like that all the time!

If only we could *be* like that all the time! For this is the crux of the matter — that in these moments of greater co-ordination we veritably are different people, in the sense that our total pattern of behaviour has unconsciously altered. It is noteworthy that the feeling of heightened physical efficiency at these times is always accompanied by a corresponding increase in mental control, which means that less work is being done to greater effect by the total mind-body mechanism.

Now whatever the underlying mental or physical causes on any particular occasion, there are always two physical events which take place, which may be detected by an experienced observer. Firstly, there is an alteration in the balance of muscular activity, which means that some muscles which previously tensed, now relax, and others which previously relaxed, now tense. Secondly, there is a subtle change in the total posture of the individual concerned, visible as a slight alteration of the relationship of the head to the neck, the shoulders to the trunk, and so on throughout the body. The latter manifestation is the more important, because it determines the operation of the former. In fact, the total posture is the determining factor in the pattern of behaviour, and without any alteration in the posture there can be no improvement in the capacity for co-ordination.

But what do we mean by 'posture'? The Shorter Oxford Dictionary gives us a starting point: "The relative disposition of the various parts of anything; especially the position and *carriage* of the limbs and the body *as a whole*". (My italics) Unfortunately, many text books on piano playing use the term 'posture' when they mean only 'position', usually in connection with such vague remarks as: "The elbow should be level with the keys", or "Sit neither too high nor too low". Certain words have been emphasised in the above definition in order to make clear that: (i) Posture includes not only 'position', but also the way in which the parts are maintained in position; (ii) The human body is an indivisible entity, in which the behaviour of any single part is dependent on the relationship existing between all the parts. Posture is therefore a totality which must take into account both the position and condition of its components, because the condition of one part modifies the position of its adjacent parts, and *vice versa*, throughout the whole structure. (The terms 'position' and 'condition' may also be interchanged or used in combination in this statement.)

A simple illustration of this concept was given by some correspondence which appeared in *The Guardian* some years ago, concerning motorists who experienced stiff necks after prolonged periods of driving. Some were able to remove the condition by adjusting their driving position, other found that such an adjustment merely transferred the stiffness to another part of the body, whilst a third category of motorists found that they were unable to remove the tension no matter what position they adopted; they resorted to such expedients as shaking the head and other 'relaxation' exercises in order to afford themselves temporary relief.

Neck tensions are often the bane of pianists as well as motorists, even though their existence may only be realised when they begin to cause actual physical discomfort. They are one manifestation of a general maldistribution of muscular tensions stemming from postural deficiency, of which the inevitable consequence is a reduction in one's capacity for co-ordination. It follows that those motorists who do not incur stiff necks after long spells at the wheel must *ipso facto* be the better drivers, just as those who feel no strain when accomplishing even the most demanding tasks at the keyboard must be the better pianists — because of the postural conditions which they enjoy.

Fluctuations in capacity for co-ordination may therefore be equated with changes in the total posture, albeit so slight that the individual concerned is unaware of them, but sufficient to alter the whole balance of muscular activity with regard to the performance of a given task, such as playing the piano. Tobias Matthay suggested that these fluctuations in ability were probably due to variations in the amount of 'muscle-tone', i.e. the amount of tension still remaining in a muscle when it has reached the point of maximum relaxation. But he did not bother to enquire into the reasons, dismissing the whole question as being of no pedagogic importance since there was nothing one could do about it.* There is, in fact, a great deal which one can do about it, and to raise the general level of the student's

* Matthay, T. *Piano Fallacies of Today,* p. 8 (O.U.P. 1939)

talent, so that his days 'on form' become the rule rather than the exception, is a task of far greater pedagogic importance than showing him how to rotate his fore- arm or 'equalise' his fingers.

At this point the reader may well ask: "You say that the posture determines the balance of muscular act- ivity. Could it not be the other way round?"

The answer is that both factors are mutually depen- dent and any alteration of the posture is impossible without a redistribution of the muscular tensions which maintain it. But it must be remembered that, by defini- tion, posture includes not only the relationship of the parts, but also what may be termed the 'static' balance of muscular activity which controls this relationship. Therefore when work is actually done, as in depressing a piano key, the amount to which some muscles relax and others tense is determined by the total posture, which includes the balance of muscular activity already prevailing.

The indivisibility of mind and body cannot be over- emphasised. Psychic tensions can create neck tensions which in their turn have a deleterious influence on the general posture. It is unlikely that all the motorists mentioned earlier suffered from stiff necks solely be- cause their driving positions accentuated pre-existing postural deficiencies; research has shown that motor- ing is a type of 'stress situation', to which all drivers unconsciously react in one way or another. Conversely, neck tensions created physically will diminish mental awareness and alertness, as anyone who cares to experi- ment by pulling the head back or hunching the shoulders for a few minutes, will discover.

There are many different schools of Yoga, but their disciplines are all based on the same principle — the integration of mind and body. Only recently in Western civilisation have we begun to realise the indivisibility of the mind-body mechanism, for instance in the recognition that psychic tensions may express themselves as physical tensions and *vice versa.*

Let us return to the case of the student who has experienced a sudden gain in his capacity for co-ordination. Perhaps the prime cause was a release of psychic tension, maybe the result of receiving some good news, or a decision taken, or something of that nature.

The release of psychic tension would have expressed itself as a release of physical tensions which would have reacted on the total posture sufficiently to ensure that the student made a better use of himself when he came to play the piano. On the other hand, our student may have adjusted himself by mainly physical means, for example, a brisk walk or a particularly well-digested meal. Whatever the initial cause, an alteration in the total posture is the immediate cause of any improvement in co-ordination. Posture is therefore the key to the problem of talent.

Sergei Rachmaninoff aged 11

3 'Expansion' *versus* 'Contraction'

For the purposes of analysis, I shall identify two basic postural conditions — the 'contracting' and the 'expanding', which may be described as the 'negative' and 'positive' poles of the total posture. The use of the present participle is deliberate, as posture is in reality dynamic, though for purposes of description we must treat it as if it were static. It must be understood that there is no neutral state of posture; when the conditions of expansion are present, the conditions of contraction are in abeyance and *vice versa*.

In the contracting posture, one tends to become shorter and narrower, because the joint surfaces are drawn towards each other by opposing muscular tensions. Here is a simple experiment which illustrates this idea:

Stand facing a wall at such a distance that when the arm is held out horizontally, with the palm of the hand facing the floor, the finger tips are just touching the wall. Flex the arm quickly at the elbow, bringing the back of the hand up to the shoulder, hold it firmly in this position for a moment, then return the arm to the horizontal position. If you have contracting tendencies, you will find that the fingers no longer touch the wall, the arm seeming to have shortened by as much as an inch or two. Imagine this condition existing throughout the entire body in a greater or lesser degree — such is the contracting posture.

Unfortunately, one's posture tends to be so habitual that one is unaware of the conditions subsisting. With regard to the dynamic aspect, it is interesting to note that the records kept by tailors of customers' measurements over the years often bear witness to the shortening of stature which actually takes place under the influence of the contracting posture. Its extreme manifestations are as follows: neck tensions which pull the head back and thrust the chin forward, rigid, pulled-back shoulders, narrow prominent shoulder blades and a pronounced hollow in the small of the back, showing that the dorsal vertebrae are contracted towards each other.

Muscles perform two functions: either of shortening the tendons to which they are attached (tensing) or of allowing the tendons to lengthen (relaxing). In a strictly scientific sense, there is no such thing as relaxation, only varying degrees of tension, and it must be realised that relaxing is just as much a function of muscular activity as tensing. Moreover, muscles are arranged in pairs, so that in co-ordinated activity, balance and control are achieved by one set of muscles contracting whilst the other set lengthens, as for example, the flexors and extensors ('benders' and 'stretchers') of the various joints of the arm.

In the experiment described above, any shortening of the arm which takes place is due to the simultaneous contraction of opposing muscles. Not only do the extensors of the forearm refuse to relax at the same rate as the flexors contract when the arm is bent at the elbow, but it will be found that the neck and shoulder muscles, not even required for the task in hand, are also in this state of hypertension, which is the root cause of all mal-co-ordinated gestures. There is no such thing as purely localised muscular activity; the shortening of the arm cannot take place without the involuntary contraction of the neck and shoulder muscles. The arm may be restored to its original condition by shaking it and letting it fall. (This is analogous to a pianist practising 'relaxation' exercises, a temporary expedient which has no lasting effect if he is fundamentally in a contracting postural condition). The shortening of the arm which occurs under contracting conditions is the result of all the joint surfaces involved being drawn towards each other.

A person who is in an expanding postural condition, which tends towards co-ordination, will not be able to shorten the arm in the above experiment unless he deliberately wills an excess of tension in the arm and shoulder. In the expanding posture, the tendency is to become longer and wider, as the joint surfaces separate away from each other. The head is well balanced on the neck, whose muscles are in minimum tension, the shoulders are loose and wide in relation to the back so that the arms tend to hang towards the front of the body, and there is no pronounced hollow in the small of the back caused by hypertension in the muscles of the dorsal vertebrae. Another noticeable difference between the two extremes of posture is that those who are in the expanding posture are 'deep' breathers, those in the contracting posture are 'shallow' breathers, factors which have obviously important effects on general physical efficiency. Without exception, it is from the ranks of the posturally expanded that all the great instrumental and vocal talents are drawn, as the reader may verify from his own observation. The required head, neck and shoulder relationship is clearly shown in the portraits of child prodigies reproduced in this book.

In the expanding posture, the tendency is towards
correct muscular equilibrium, in which every muscle
performs only the task it should perform, whether of
tensing or relaxing, to the extent required, which is the
sine qua non of any co-ordinated activity. For example,
let us take the apparently simple activity of maintaining
the head on the neck, in sitting or standing upright.
If the activity is co-ordinated, the head will be balanced
on the neck by the tension in the sub-occipital muscles
at the top of the spine and the complementary lengthening of the trapezius and sterno-mastoid muscles. But
in the contracting posture, where the force of gravity
is overcome by mal-co-ordinated means, the large neck
muscles are forced to contract — the very opposite of
the function which they ought to perform.

If we consider the elementary pianistic activity of
bringing the hand into playing position on the keyboard, the different results achieved under these opposing postural conditions are even more obvious. The
'expanding' person merely brings the arm forward from
his wide and forward-tending shoulder and the hand
falls naturally into place on the keys. If a 'contracting'
person were to perform the same gesture in relation to
his backward-tending shoulder, the only finger in
contact with the keys would be the fifth, with the
others lying on top of it. In practice, a series of adjustments is made unconsciously to bring the hand into
position, of necessity involving contrary exertions
which manifest themselves as stiffness at the elbow
and shoulder joint. The playing positions arrived at by
either means may appear identical to the eye; if one
checks for mobility at the elbow by the use of touch,
the freedom of movement enjoyed by the 'expanding'
player as opposed to the inhibited condition of his
'contracted' colleague is immediately obvious, even
before any playing activity takes place.

My discussion so far has been confined to some physical aspects of posture which are capable of external observation. Unfortunately, the implications of posture in the sphere of mental activity can only be experienced. As Tobias Matthay wrote: "Musical alertness and technical freedom certainly seem to go hand in hand, and Body and Mind, it is manifest, always react on each other".*

However, a great deal can be learnt from the following experiment:

Place a matchbox or other small object on a table in front of you and try to pick it up as slowly as possible. The harder you concentrate on slowing down the operation, the more conscious you will become of increasing mental and physical tension.

Now repeat the experiment in this way:

Imagine yourself as a detached observer of the operation. Instead of concentrating directly on the task in hand, merely *see* the arm moving slowly out from the body, merely *see* the hand closing over the matchbox and so on.

It will be found that in this apparently dissociated manner of performance there is a far greater tendency towards co-ordination. There is not only a decrease in the amount of mental and physical tension involved, but a corresponding increase in control over the performance.

In the first method of performance, concentration on the end to be gained interferes with the radar-like workings of the kinetic mechanism, inducing contracting tendencies which manifest themselves as a deterioration of the posture. In the second method of performance, where one refuses to concentrate directly on the end to be gained, this kind of inter-

*Matthay, T. *op. cit.* p.8

ference is reduced to a minimum, which at least prevents a deterioration in whatever capacity for co-
ordination one may originally possess. The important point to grasp is that this second method of performance, here adopted consciously, is the way in which
one tends to perform naturally and unconsciously under
the influence of the expanding posture. As Artur
Schnabel once remarked, in a typical paradox: "The
secret of successful performance lies in absolute concentration on absolute relaxation".

Schnabel was of course speaking of the mental
aspect of performing. If the argument of this book
has been understood so far, it will be realised that for
the great talents, this is the only aspect which matters.
Discussing Liszt's *B minor Sonata*, Magaloff said:
"So many pianists 'get busy' with a work like this.
They think: "Here come the big chords . . . now for the
octaves . . . ." and so on. *I simply follow the line of
the music*". Gieseking said: "The only thing I find
necessary is to form an absolutely clear picture of
how the work should go", and similar remarks have
been made by other eminent artists.

Unfortunately, so many pianists are trained to
'get busy' for so long that even if they arrive at an over-
all conception of the work they wish to perform, their
technical habits interfere with its realisation. In extreme
cases, the performer becomes little more than the slave
of his fingers. He works at his pieces until he has acquired
a set of conditioned reflexes, responding to the stimulus
of performance like one of Pavlov's dogs salivating at
the sound of a bell. Unfortunately, the process which
conditions the fingers conditions the mind at the same
time, with ruinous artistic consequences. That 'art' can
be divorced from 'technique' is a delusion. Furthermore, technique is divorced even further from the
reality of actual music-making by being divided into

different compartments, one mechanism for finger passages, another for thirds, another for octaves, etc., so that the busy pianist is constantly practising the very opposite of that simple continuous flow of gesture with which the talented performer follows the line of a work. The principle of 'divide and conquer' may have some validity in those branches of education which are concerned with 'knowing' rather than 'doing', but in the education of the performer 'integrate to co-ordinate' should be the battle-cry.

Reality disappears further over the horizon when we consider the multiplicity of technical treatises and methods which have been published and practised during the past century, many of them so contradictory as to cancel each other out. If Professor 'X's theories are right, then Professor 'Y's must be wrong. How is it, therefore, that Professor 'Y's pupils not only manage to play at all, but also manage to play as well as those of Professor 'X'?

This was one of the problems which exercised Professor Thiberge as early as 1903. In the following chapter we shall see how he tackled it and how he was led to some of his far-reaching conclusions on the nature of piano performance which have been incorporated into this book.

Ferrucio Busoni aged 12

4 The Researches of Raymond Thiberge

A colleague who teaches singing once remarked: "The best that one can say about most methods of voice production is that some are less destructive than others". Fortunately, that remark could never apply so forcibly to piano teaching, for even when subjected to the worst possible 'methods', the hands and fingers are capable of standing up to much more punishment than the vocal mechanism. Even so, the talented pianist often succeeds in spite of the tuition he has received, and not because of it.

Professor Thiberge's researches began because he had sufficient humility to realise that the successes of his more talented pupils did not necessarily prove the validity of his teaching methods, which ran along traditional lines at that time; he refused to assume that because his methods worked for these pupils, the failures of the others could only be blamed on their lack of talent. In his own words: "During my early years as a piano teacher, I became increasingly disturbed by the following problem: Why were the results obtained by certain conscientious and hard-working students so mediocre in comparison with the effort expended?

Determined to unravel this mystery, I made a careful study of most of the numerous books which were published on the piano technique even in those days, and finally sought out the authors of some of these works: some from what is commonly called the 'arm-weight' or 'relaxationist' school, others from the 'fixationist' camp.

But these meetings, far from dissipating my worries, only made them more acute. Being deprived of sight, I had to place my hands on the arms of my mentors in order to comprehend the procedures of which they were giving examples. To my great astonishment, my hands revealed to me that their technical procedures were actually in disagreement with the principles which they professed!

In pursuing my researches with the aid of touch, the sole means at my disposal, I began to realise how difficult it is to be conscious of one's *real* gestures when performing, and how much teaching operates solely by hypotheses, making different deductions from the same effect, because the true cause is not directly perceivable.

Traditional teaching is often led astray by observing only effects, then by deduction, determining artibrarily the causes. This systematic error has falsified the bases of musical education, and is the real reason behind so many of the 'difficulties' encountered in the elementary as well as the advanced stages of the pianist's development".*

So he discovered that the authors of some apparently authoritative books on piano technique were deceiving both themselves and their readers because they took for granted the validity of their purely subjective feelings as to how they were using themselves in the act of playing the piano.

It was then that Thiberge realised where the answers

* Thiberge, R. *Le Pianiste*, p. 12 (Editions LecVire, Vire 1951)

lay to his problems — in a careful tactile observation *free from all pre-conceived notions*, of the conditions actually subsisting in his own students, just as Froebel had realised in the previous century that education should be based on a study of the child. Froebel's ideas were considered highly revolutionary in their time, although they do not appear to be very extraordinary in the twentieth century. However 'revolutionary' some of Thiberge's ideas may seem to be at first sight, it must be borne in mind that they are not hypotheses, but statements of *verifiable fact* concerning the use of the human mechanism in playing the piano.

The first question which he investigated was that of 'relaxation', which has aroused more controversy than any other amongst piano teachers. Undoubtedly the greater proportion of students seem to feel the need for relaxation exercises in one form or another, and their teachers feel the necessity of prescribing them. But why should these exercises only be felt to be necessary in connection with playing the piano? Is there a special kind of suppleness required for pianists and does the practising of 'relaxation' exercises promote it?

Thiberge noticed how often the clumsiness of so many of his beginners was not apparent when they made gestures unrelated to piano playing, and how often the stiffness of their arms, hands and fingers disappeared when the arm was withdrawn from the keyboard. Could it be that these pupils were destroying their own natural suppleness by the way in which they made contact with the keyboard?

Thiberge came to the conclusion that the answer to this question was undoubtedly in the affirmative. As to whether 'relaxation' exercises help to promote suppleness, he points out that whereas the prolonged stretching of a piece of rubber may reduce its powers of contraction, the continued lengthening of a muscle does not prevent it from contracting again, immediately it is required to do so. But in any case, to relax is just as normal a function of muscular activity as to contract. The equation of suppleness with muscular relaxation stems from the false hypothesis that suppleness, together with many other factors in piano technique, has a purely muscular basis. To try to create suppleness in the muscles is to attempt to create a possibility which already exists, a waste of time which should be devoted to more constructive purposes.

It must be remembered that suppleness is a purely negative attribute: — freedom from stiffness, and the origins of stiffness are not to be found in any deficiencies in the workings of the muscles, which are probably the most efficient and flexible organs we possess, but solely in contrary exertions, which are the cause of mal-co-ordinated gestures.

One of the most interesting examples of a contrary exertion discovered by Thiberge was that of the shoulder attempting to draw the upper arm backwards in the act of raising the arm to the keyboard. This is a very common phenomenon, even amongst those who do not possess any markedly contracting postural tendencies. It is usually unnoticeable to the eye, but may easily be detected by the use of touch.

To give a complete list of the contrary and even contradictory exertions which the body is capable of making would be an almost impossible task. Nor would it be a very profitable one, since there is no point in discussing them in isolation. In the words of Professor Thiberge: "As all the parts of the body are so intimately bound up with each other, the entire body of the pianist is capable of giving rise to exertions which are destructive to the suppleness of the fingers, and for that matter, the suppleness of the limbs in general".

With regard to the technicalities of performance,

precisely the same conclusions may be drawn, that clumsiness in general, and technical failures in particular, have no other origins than in the making of simultaneous contradictory gestures.

Here is one example, out of the innumerable possibilities provided by the fingers, hand, arm and shoulder acting in conjunction: to depress a piano key in front of one by means of the finger is to make a gesture in one direction; to pull the upper arm backwards at the same time is to make a gesture in a contrary direction, which neutralises the efficiency of the gesture of key-depression.

Of course, in slow tempo, one can use almost any means one likes in order to produce the desired musical result, but in rapid textures even the slightest complication of gesture can prove disastrous. Mal-co-ordinated gestures are fundamentally complex, co-ordinated gestures are fundamentally simple. As Thiberge says: "The superiority of the virtuosi stems less from their exceptional faculties than from the extremely simple and natural means which they have discovered of using them".

The real problem of piano technique, therefore, lies not in breaking down the resistance of the keyboard, but in eliminating the causes of interference which lie within oneself. To end this brief survey of Professor Thiberge's approach to the problem, we give one final quotation which shows how closely his ideas relate to those of Matthias Alexander: "As they are quite unaware of the errors they commit, many students may have to submit to a complete re-education of the way in which they use their faculties. Only when one is engaged in this kind of work can one realise the enormous extent to which the majority of people are incapable of making the fullest use of their potentialities.

Piano teaching, as I understand it, should help to

remedy this situation. It serves not only musical education, but the education of human beings in their entirety.

The well-being of one's muscular and articulatory
faculties delivers one from illness. If technical difficulties vary with the individual, just as illnesses differ
from person to person, piano technique and good health
have one point in common: normal function. The
teacher, like the doctor, must treat the various patients
who are submitted to him, from the point of view of
restoring them to this unity: normal functioning."

Following this splendid precept, the remaining
chapters of this book are devoted to outlining the means
by which the growth of co-ordination may be achieved
in the individual and maintained during performance.
Hardly any discussion will be found of the usual technical problems, because these tend to wither away as
one's capacity for co-ordination grows, when one
begins to realise the full significance of this remark,
made by one of the most talented pianists of recent
times: "I never knew piano playing was so difficult
until I tried to teach it".

Alfred Cortot aged 11

5 "Vous êtes bien assis?"

This question was invariably asked by Cortot before his students began to play. How one sits is vitally important, because it affects everything one does at the keyboard. In the 'hand touching wall' experiment outlined in Chapter 4, it will be remembered that the means used in standing determined the result. Similarly, the means used in sitting, whether contracting or expanding, will determine the efficiency or otherwise of one's performing gestures. In this chapter we shall describe the requirements of sitting by expanding means and furthermore a means of using ourselves when seated which actually develops the expanding posture, *sine qua non* of the flowering of whatever talent we possess for playing the piano.

Our first requirement is a chair with a smooth, flat bottom and a straight back. The back of the chair is not for leaning on, it merely provides a check-point. A firm seat is essential at any time, since any reduction in the chair's efficiency as a gravity-resister has to be compensated for by muscular activity. One should never sit on cushions in order to play the piano. To every action, there is an equal and opposite reaction, therefore the resistance of the seat must at least equal that of the piano mechanism under its heaviest stress. Any failure of resistance on the part of the chair is instinctively redressed by harmful bodily contractions.

The correct technique of sitting is very simple: one stands comfortably balanced in front of the chair and then allows the knees and ankles to bend — and nothing else to happen. We allow the force of gravity to draw the body downwards in a controlled surrender which helps it to remain 'long' at the same time. Under these conditions, extraneous contractions are as redundant as buttresses to a properly balanced wall. One neither collapses into the chair nor maintains one's equilibrium through opposing tensions on either side of the centre of gravity, as in the common case of those who thrust their buttocks backwards in order to sit, which they counterbalance by thrusting the chin forward at the same time. Some people actually sit on the bottom of the spine; others manage to sit on the thighs, but force themselves into such contortions of the dorsal vertebrae in the process that they resemble a letter 's'. Whether one sits like 'r' for 'relaxation' or 's' for stiffness, the result is the same: mal-co-ordination.

For those who are habituated to sitting incorrectly, a good preliminary exercise is to stand with one's back against a smooth wall and slide the back down the wall by allowing the knees to bend facing slightly outwards. You should slide far enough to feel the small of the back contact the wall. Then straighten the legs to regain the standing position, keeping the small of the back in contact with the wall for as long as possible. You may even straighten the legs to the extent of going right up on the toes before repeating the exercise. You should soon become conscious of the balance of the head being over the feet and not behind them, i.e. that the head is 'forward and up' in Alexander's phrase, and also realise how it is possible to 'let go' the buttocks, so that the spine 'lengthens' and the back is allowed to flatten against the wall without any exertion. (The back will never totally flatten, as human beings are not made that way, and any exertion to make it so would be self-defeating).

Returning to the chair, the problem which immediately confronts the novice is one of faith. As he approaches the chair correctly for the first time, he will feel that it is no longer there to receive him! This is one of the most important lessons to be learnt with regard to the re-education of behaviour patterns — that our feelings are not to be trusted. The judgements we make as to how we operate and our sense of spatial relationships are governed entirely by our habitual usage. If a pattern is changed, disorientation ensues until a new set of associations is established. In the meantime, one refers automatically to one's habitual sensory expectations — hence the feeling of the 'disappearing' chair.

This is the moment to emphasise the necessity of the teacher. Because of the subjectivity involved, a student working alone, even after studying all the available literature and having a perfectly clear conception of what is required, may still lead himself up a blind alley without the guiding hand of an experienced teacher. Text-books can only point the way.

If the student can overcome this temporary doubt about the presence of the chair and lower himself all the way without disturbing his alignment, he will find that he is only sitting on the front edge of it. This is because at this stage I have omitted an additional requirement of normal sitting, i.e. allowing the hips to go back as well as the knees to bend, as being too complex a task for a beginner to accomplish without the danger of contracting. Once the remainder of the work outlined in this chapter has been successfully accomplished, this completion of the act of sitting should present no problem. In the meantime, one can slide oneself into the back of the chair by raising the ankles from the floor and pushing against the balls of the feet, taking care, of course, that nothing is disturbed in the process.

Taking stock at this point, it will be noticed that not only does the back feel longer than usual, but also that there is a feeling of space between the head and the body, which indicates an improvement in the head-neck-shoulder relationship. Here is a simple test which demonstrates both the importance of the balance of the head and also the interdependence of head, neck and shoulders: place the right hand on the left shoulder, or vice-versa, and note that the slightest movement of the head causes an alteration in the state of the muscles surrounding the shoulder. If you experiment with slight alterations of the balance of the head, you will be able to discover the precise head position which reduces the pull on the shoulder muscles to a minimum. You may feel that the head is out of alignment in this position and that you are no longer looking straight ahead. This will be a measure of the amount of habitual misalignment which has previously occurred, and another example of the subjectivity of our feelings which has already been discussed.

Next comes the problem of 'widening'. The ideal is to become posturally expanded to the extent that the shoulder blades are flattened out behind the collar bone, which is essential for our subsequent work at the keyboard. Here again, we make use of the force of gravity. If the body is inclined sufficiently forward at the hips, the weight of the arms will draw the shoulders away from each other, providing they are not prevented by any contracting tendencies. If the body is then returned to the upright position, the shoulders will remain 'wide and down', provided that the expanding muscles remain engaged.

It is in ensuring these provisos are fulfilled that the really hard work begins. For many people, the tasks of taking the body backwards and forwards are extremely difficult to accomplish correctly. The idea of leaning forward is often associated with 'relaxing', i.e. letting go of the anti-gravity muscles which have been so carefully brought into play up to this point, causing an immediate take-over by the contracting tendencies which are waiting to seize the slightest opportunity of reasserting themselves. The head is pulled back into the neck, the shoulders become rigid and the small of the back is pulled in again. These tendencies are so habitual with many people that they feel uncomfortable without them; in order to feel relaxed they have to tense! Moreover, force of habit is so strong that the mere thought of leaning forward can immediately induce contracting tendencies associated with the action even though it is not carried out, just as thinking of a chord arouses tension in the muscles which perform it.

Thus we have two problems to solve simultaneously: the negative one of 'unconditioning' our prevailing conditioned reflexes and the positive one of forming new behavioural patterns. Fortunately we have one infallible tool at our disposal, indeed the only means which we possess: our conscious will. This, we exercise in a simultaneous two-pronged attack — first by a rigorous perseverance in the technique of disassociation, already described in the 'picking up a match-box' experiment of Chapter 3 and secondly, through the giving of precise mental commands to ourselves.

First, we must refuse to have anything to do with the activity of leaning forward, a refusal which we strengthen by deliberately giving ourselves the command: "Don't!" We immediately follow this by positive orders which keep the contracting muscles at bay and encourage

the activity of our expanding muscles. We order the
head 'forward and up', as already described, to maintain its balance and keep the neck long, and order the
back to lengthen from the hips upwards. It must be
re-emphasised that these are not orders to do anything
— we continue to refuse to do anything — but are
preventive orders against the intrusion of contracting
tendencies. The order is not directed to muscles, because one cannot order any particular set of muscles
to tense or relax, one can only create the conditions
under which they will act. The strongest man in the
world will not be able to demonstrate the force of his
biceps with his arms hanging limp at his sides. The
muscles have to be given work to do. The mental
orders therefore are the means of taking away work
from the wrong muscles and giving it to the right
ones.

The next stage is to continue the orders to the head
and back and to think of these orders as the actual
means by which the body may *rise* from the hips.
One may think one's weight 'upwards' so that one
eventually has the sensation of being lifted off the
hips all in one place. Thus the thought sequence is
'head forward and up, back to lengthen to raise the
body'. But wait! One must be able to sustain the
thought sufficiently to waken the long slumbering
anti-gravity muscles into action, and even then, no
great movement may take place. Much patience is
required; it is the easiest thing in the world to 'do'
it, only to find that all one has really done is to hunch
the shoulders and destroy the posture, but if the technique has been sufficiently mastered the body will
eventually begin to rise.

Of course, levitation does not actually take place!
In reality, the body begins to incline forward from the
hips, in accordance with our original intentions. In

directing our feelings towards 'raising' the body, we have simply been making intelligent use of our human capacity for self-deception. (This is not to say that we cannot look forward to the time when self-deception will wither away as genuine awareness grows. But growth is a slow process.)

We may now consciously continue the inclination until the shoulders fall forward. The back is now not only long, but 'wide' at the same time. The next problem is to bring the body back from the hips without destroying this relationship. This makes even greater demands on the anti-gravity muscles and lesser results may consequently be experienced to begin with. Here we introduce the third and last of our preventive orders, 'back to widen', to prevent the shoulders from narrowing. We want the back to widen to maintain the shoulders 'down' and to keep the head, neck and shoulder relationship in the inclined plane now existing, whilst only the small of the back is willed to come back from the hips. The contradiction implied here is only one of the imagination, another piece of self-deception which enables us to bring the body back from the hips as one unit, with the expanded relationship of its parts unimpaired.

Whether the body has been brought completely back to the vertical or not, this relationship may be sustained by giving oneself this mental order: "Head forward and up; back to lengthen and widen". The modifications which have taken place in the condition of the arms as a result of our work should now be taken note of. If the hand is placed on the thigh, it will be found to rest so lightly that only the finger tips are in contact with the thigh and all sensation of weight in the arm has disappeared. I must emphasise that this occurs not because we make any deliberate attempt to hold off our 'arm-weight', but as a natural result of the improved posture at which we have arrived.

To take up position at the piano, the arm is ordered to lengthen and is led from underneath the relaxed shoulder — not by the hand, which remains inert — to the keyboard. The hand will fall into place in an outward-facing position, with the centre of gravity lying towards the thumb side. At the same time, the elbows will be found to be away from the body and pointing outwards. If one also feels the need to sit somewhat lower and further away from the keyboard than before, this is a healthy sign. When a talented, and consequently 'expanding' performer adjusts his seat during a recital, it is always in this direction, never the opposite.

Of course there is nothing unusual about this playing position, but it will have been achieved by the most co-ordinated means possible for us at the time. Moreover, we have been working in a way which has demonstrably stimulated the growth of our capacity for co-ordination. But we must not forget that the growth is a slow process. The ultimate goal of becoming the person who has no further need of the procedures outlined above may never be reached; all that matters is that one continues to improve. Certainly through working in this way the student will come to appreciate the truth of the maxim that in order to command one's fingers, one must be able to command one's self.

Erwin Nyiregehazi aged 9

6 Co-ordination with the keyboard

Tobias Matthay based his teaching on three species of touch, together with various sub-divisions and combinations.* His most virulent opponent, the 'fixationist' James Ching, also classified piano playing according to different touch formations, and this is the common approach of most writers.**Matthay said that no other approach was possible "in the face of the doings of great Artists". It is my contention that these "doings" are not the real means of performance, but by-products, and that, much more important, the great artists have a common way of using *themselves* in order to perform. For the great talents, playing the piano is experienced as a *Gestalt*, a totality of activity enjoyed from childhood as naturally and unconsciously as any other form of play, and something to be taken for granted as other people accept the ability to walk or speak. "Quite frankly", said Arthur Rubinstein in a recent radio interview, "I don't know *how* I do it", which is as it should be.

Of course, any performance worthy of the name must present itself as a *Gestalt*, but the 'divide and conquer' theorists have never been able to explain how

*Matthay, T. *The Act of Touch, passim* (Longmans Green 1905)
**Ching, J. *Piano Playing, passim* (Bosworth 1946)

different forms of touch merge and mesh together
into a continuous whole in the act of performance,
and many have not even bothered to try. One can't
stop doing one thing then start doing another and if
the texture demands that two mutually exclusive
touches overlap, why doesn't paralysis occur at that
point? How, in fact, is continuity created?

George Woodhouse, one of the few teachers to
grapple seriously with this problem, eventually came to
this conclusion: ". . . I realised that the pianists's fingers
recorded the isolated events; his body the musical
progression. Speech and song present a near analogy.
The vocal organs are concerned with the formation of
every note, word and syllable. Each is given a complete structure of its own while the invisible mind-body
dynamic interprets the inherent tensions of thought
forms, whether speech or song"*

It is unfortunate that his traditionally conditioned
way of thinking prevented him from realising that the
"invisible mind-body dynamic" which he had discovered was not something which ran in harness with
the 'doings' of the fingers, but is in fact, the mainspring of whatever they do. Yet this is implicit in his
analogy with speech and song, where the vocal chords
are incapable of being exercised save at the behest of
the "inherent tensions of thought forms".

Furthermore, although the 'body' half of the syn-
drome may be invisible, it is nevertheless palpable and
capable of being consciously created, providing one is
in a sufficiently co-ordinated condition to be able to
do so. It is the talented performer's intuitive means
whereby he initiates and maintains a co-ordinated dia-
logue with the mechanism of his instrument.

Let us remember that to each and every action,

* Woodhouse, G. *A Realistic Approach to Piano Playing,* p. 55 (Augener
1953)

there is an equal and opposite re-action. The great virtue of the piano mechanism is its resilience, which gives such remarkable economy of effort to the performer — providing he knows how to make use of it. Those who do know, may expend far less physical effort in a whole recital than many a student expends in half-an-hour's practice. Under co-ordinated conditions nearly all the energy expended on key-depression is returned to the performer by the rebound of the key. This returned energy may be transferred to the next key depression, or used to help the arm to travel, or re-used for any combination of purposes for which it is required. For instance, the performance of rapid octaves or skips would be impossible without the co-operation of the piano mechanism. Throwing the hands in the air at a climax is not necessarily a gesture of showmanship; it can be the inevitable result of letting the piano action 'have the last word' at the end of a particularly energetic paragraph. (N.B. There is a time limit beyond which this returned energy becomes dissipated if not re-used soon enough. For example, it is necessary to make a new impulse for each chord in Chopin's *Prelude in C minor*.)

The total activity of a co-ordinated performance may therefore be expressed as a two-way flow of energy between the performer and his instrument. Paradoxically, the performer must be able to surrender to this flow in order to control it. Only when one has learnt to do this can one achieve that exhilirating experience which should be the reward of all technical endeavour — that the piano is 'playing itself'. (Thiberge gave me a taste of this at our first meeting. I played the Chopin study in thirds from opus 25. After various manipulations and adjustments came the startling injunction: "Stop trying to play the piano with your fingers!" and the less I did, the better the playing became.)

Allied to the reduction of effort which stems from
co-ordination is the healthy feeling of elasticity engendered in the arms, hands and fingers, which are
felt to be as resilient as the piano mechanism itself.
This is an illusion, of course, because the arms contain
no springs, tendons are not made of rubber, and bones
are totally inflexible. Side by side with the illusion of
elasticity, described in one way or another by many
virtuosi from Thalberg onwards, has gone the other
illusion that touch influences the quality of tone.
Both these myths have been exploded by modern
scientific research, notably that of Otto Ortmann in the
Physical Basis of Piano Touch and Tone (New York
1925) and *The Physiological Mechanics of Piano Technique* (New York 1929), which led to a vogue for
teaching piano playing as a branch of mechanics, as
exemplified in the work of James Ching in England.
Fortunately, the real artists of the keyboard have
continued to be guided by their illusions, since the
mechanistic approach does not take into account the
true nature of the relationship of the talented performer
to his instrument. (Discussing touch and tone in 1948,
when the 'scientific' approach was at the height of
fashion, Schnabel said: "Of course the piano is a mechanical instrument; it will respond to your intentions
with amazing accuracy and precision. *Play it in a mechanical way and you will get a mechanical result",* which
says all that needs to be said on this subject, as far as
the musician is concerned.)

The talented performer literally expands in order to
play. If he does not, he must perforce contract. As we
have seen earlier, there is no neutral effort, and contracting procedures which are inimical to co-ordination
are not the means whereby talent expresses itself. In
concrete terms, the 'invisible mind-body dynamic'
which participates with the piano mechanism in creating

the flow of energy of a performance is a single, simple gesture of expansion which operates throughout the total posture, to which all other gestures are related either as by-products or adaptive adjustments.

Ortmann himself said: "The whole neural system is opposed to isolated or disintegrated action. The smallest movement of piano technique as used in actual playing involves, actively or passively, the trunk as well as the arm, hand and fingers",* but he, like Woodhouse, could not make the necessary mental leap which would have taken this discovery to its logical conclusion. Thiberge discovered the gesture of expansion because of his determination to rid himself of all pre-conceived notions in pursuing his researches.

The student in his turn must rid himself of pre-conceived notions in his pursuit of the elusive ideal of perfect co-ordination with the keyboard. He must first of all get rid of the notion that because the fingers are in direct contact with the keys, they are the instruments of tone-production. This is a confusion of ends and means, and to operate the fingers directly is an 'end-gaining' procedure, in Alexander's phrase, which actually conspires against gaining possession of the 'means whereby'. (That it is the happy lot of great talents to be only concerned with the 'ends' does not invalidate the statement. To paraphrase T.S. Eliot, "we must arrive at where they start".) The fingers are the links in the chain of co-ordination, which not only transmit and receive energy to and from the keys, but also perform miracles of high-speed adaptation to the contours of the keyboard according to the demands of the music. The efficiency with which they perform this latter task will depend entirely on their innate suppleness, i.e. freedom from contrary exertions.

* Ortmann, O. *The Physiological Mechanics of Piano Technique*, p. 71 (Kegan Paul 1929)

To preserve maximum suppleness in the fingers, on which co-ordination with the keyboard depends, we must remove from them the burden of being treated as active agents in the act of tone production and instead regard them solely as transmitters of our basic gesture of expansion.

Here is a simple experiment, which although crude in comparison with the finesse required for piano playing, nevertheless gives a valid experience of the nature of the gesture of postural expansion:

Having regard to the correct postural conditions outlined in the previous chapter, sit opposite an open door. Your position should be such that when you bring the arm into 'playing position', you can contact the door with one finger, not very far away from the hinge so that the door presents some resistance to the finger. Check with the free hand that all the joints of the operating arm are mobile, as they should be if you have maintained your co-ordination in the act of presenting the finger to the door. The problem is simply to close the door with maximum control over the operation with regard to speed and force, using only the contact of the fingertip. (So we are using the door as a crude substitute for a piano key.) Furthermore, no matter how much force is applied, the joints of the arm, hand and fingers must continue to remain supple. You will quickly discover that maximum control over the operation can only be achieved by the use of pressure, and that directing one's effort solely through the finger or arm will result in certain failure with regard to the maintenance of suppleness. The only solution to the problem is to work to the other end so that the whole chain of expanding muscles throughout the body will be brought into operation. Order the back to lengthen to engage the contraction of the muscles of the upper part of the thigh (*Quadraceps femoris*). This will suffice to induce an expansion throughout the posture which will be felt equally against the door and against the seat of the chair. If the gesture is correctly made (and it must be realised that a very precise alignment of the body together with a high degree of awareness, is required) the pressure against the door may be as much as one cares to make it, but the wrist and elbow joints will still remain free. If the arm is pushed upwards, downwards or sideways with the free hand, no resistance should be encountered.

This then, is the gesture of expansion discovered by Raymond Thiberge, which the reader may discover for himself by means of the somewhat crude experiment outlined above. Even though we are only pressing against a door, the subtlety and elusive nature of the gesture and the finesse of co-ordination required will have been realised. Some fortunate readers may find that they can perform the operation correctly without any conscious expansion whatsoever. Nevertheless, it is still there, as may be discovered by the exercise of a very high degree of awareness and checking with the free hand on top of the thigh, where it is most obtrusive. In the next chapter we shall see how postural expansion operates at the keyboard and also test the validity of this statement: that since it is the only means of making a sound which demands total co-ordination within the performer and with his instrument, it is the only 'touch' we need to practise in order to improve our technique in general.

(This is the moment to point out the close relationship which exists between pianism and the art of dancing. In fact, the whole argument of the preceding pages is summarised in this analogy: *The pianist uses the keyboard as the dancer uses the floor.* One does not need movement training to discover that to take one's first dance step requires an initial invisible gesture of expansion. From then on, the floor becomes the mainspring of movement as long as expansion is maintained. Without expansion, there is no dance, only shuffling or stamping. To study the relationship between pianism and dancing in all its correspondences is a highly rewarding exercise, unfortunately beyond the scope of this book. Here I can only say that such terms as 'support', 'gesture', 'free flow' and others commonly used in the art of movement, provide an intelligible vocabulary of the principles of piano playing as I understand it, although in writing this book I have preferred to avoid using technical language as far as possible.)

Raymond Thiberge in 1940

7 The Teaching of Raymond Thiberge

The liberation of talent must proceed on two fronts:
(a) The improvement of posture and general co-ordination.
(b) The elimination of contracting procedures as the means of performance and the substitution of expanding ones.

As we have suggested, victory on the second front can only be gained by the total disregard of any means of tone-production save that of the gesture of postural expansion described in the previous chapter. This was all that Thiberge taught. Forced by blindness to work entirely empirically and literally in the dark, he nevertheless deduced these basic requirements, expressed in his own terms as: "correct alignment of the segments of bone structure in a condition of balanced muscular activity", (in which his findings coincide precisely with those of Alexander on the question of posture), and *"la pression"*. His theory was that once the segments of the bone structure were correctly organised, a pressure initiated by "a subtle gesture of leverage against the thigh" could be transmitted through them to the finger-tips without any intervening contractions. This was his own anatomically implausible, but experientially valid description of the gesture of expansion acting

throughout the total posture, which will be translated
as 'the pressure' in the rest of this book for the sake of
convenience. Any reversion to the everyday meaning
of 'pressure' should be immediately obvious from the
context.

The greatness of Thiberge's teaching lay in his recognition that the ability to make one single sound by
genuinely co-ordinated means was worth more to the
artistic growth of his students than showing them how
to negotiate the supposed 'difficulties of the music'
by the employment of any manner of 'end-gaining'
methods. My first six lessons with him were devoted to
playing no more than a C major scale in double octaves.
In the first lesson, I never got beyond the first note.
There is no substitute for work, but in the long run,
only the quality of the work matters, not the quantity.

The following account of a lesson with Professor
Thiberge gives an idea of the quality of the work which
must be undertaken by anyone sufficiently motivated
towards the re-education of their pianistic faculties. The
aim of the lesson is to perform a scale of C major in
octaves with the right hand.

First, Thiberge checks that the pupil is sitting on the
thighs and that the pelvis and knee joints are mobile.
(The feet are not extended to the pedals to begin with,
but are kept underneath the knees. Later, when balance
is well-established, the left foot will still remain for
support whilst the right is pedalling.) Now comes a
little of what may be described as "Thiberge
Technique":

The pupil is encouraged to 'let go' the arm completely so that Thiberge can take hold of it and place
it into the desired relationship with the keyboard and
the shoulder. By the way in which he raises the arm,
the shoulder is encouraged to 'widen' at the same time,
so that the shoulder blade fans outwards and flattens,

forming what Thiberge calls a *fourche de cheval* with the collar bone. The arm is then brought into line with the keyboard with the point of the elbow tending outwards and the wrist tending in the opposite direction. The task of the pupil is merely to be aware of what the conditions are and to concentrate on doing nothing at all, especially not 'helping' the teacher in any way. (The temptation to 'do' is unfortunately so strong in most people that only the exercise of the most acute self-awareness will suffice to keep it at bay. As Thiberge says: "To do nothing is one of the hardest tasks in the world.")

He then checks that the arm is correctly aligned with the shoulder by taking hold of the pupil's hand and exerting a gentle pressure in the direction of the elbow. If the arm-shoulder relationship is correct, the elbow will not move backwards, and the pressure will be felt against the shoulder. Thiberge then suggests that the pupil may resist his pressure by means of a slight exertion against the thigh. This of course is the gesture of expansion. The difficulty here is that the pupil will fail to appreciate just how little effort is required and will do anything but the one simple thing which is demanded of him. The effort against the thigh is hardly more than a thought. In fact, one should not attempt to make it directly, but rather to think of it as 'being done' and that the combination of forces arising from his pressure and one's own would result in the body tending upwards and backwards. The arm would lengthen, the body would lengthen, and the angle at the hips would tend to widen, i.e. a general expansion would take place.

Thiberge then takes the pupil's hand and gently depresses an octave with the thumb and fifth finger. The pupil takes no part whatsoever in the act of key-depression. He is then requested to maintain the key in its depressed position by means of the pressure which he has already experienced. So the situation is that the pupil's fingers, arms and hand are quite 'dead' and the upthrust of the key is being contained by the expansion of the total posture. The sensation is one of immediate awareness of the pressure against the keys — a oneness of the body and finger-tips. In the words of one student "There doesn't feel to be anything between the finger-tips and shoulder". The reason for this sensation is the absence of certain tensions habitually associated with the act of key depression, which of course is why Thiberge does all the work for the student up to this point. If you are an habitual 'wrong-doer', you cannot possibly know what it feels to 'do right'. You have to learn to do nothing in order that you may be made aware of the new sensations associated with 'right-doing' — a principle which also lies at the heart of Alexander's teaching.

Although the arm feels very relaxed, and mobile in every direction except that of the line of force between key and shoulder, nevertheless the 'expanding' muscles will be in tension. Particularly noticeable should be those on the outside of the upper arm, those just above the hip, and the thigh muscles already mentioned. At the same time, the inside of the arm and the underneath part of the thighs should feel soft owing to the absence of tension in the 'contracting' muscles.

If all has gone well so far, work can begin on the octave scale, which has to be played *as legato as possible in one continuous gesture*. This task is chosen by Raymond Thiberge because it demands the finest possible co-ordination for its accomplishment. Unlike a five-finger exercise, one can't 'get away with it'. Everything has to be right, otherwise there will be no travel at all or no *legato*. Of course the only continuous tone-producing gesture one can make between one key and the next is a *glissando*; all else (save for the continuity of the hidden gesture of expansion) is illusion, although not necessarily illusory in terms of pyscho-somatic experience, which is all that matters to the artist.

The following examples show that we begin with descending passages in the right hand, *vice-versa* for the left, which are easier for the maintenance of the arm adjustment in the first instance, than those in the opposite direction. The short groups are used as 'practise runs' for the full scales. The first pause in each example indicates Thiberge's depression of the keys; the second pause indicates the taking over by the pupil of the maintenance of key depression by means of the gesture of expansion:

L.H. 'mirror' opposite

In performing the scale, the *tempo* must not be too slow, otherwise it will break down into a series of isolated impulses. (If the *tempo* is too fast, *staccato* emerges, c.f. the note on *staccato* playing in Chapter 9). The problem is to convert the static energy employed in containing the upthrust of the key into kinetic energy, using the means already at our disposal and *only those means*. Although a great complexity of interactions will take place between the playing apparatus and the piano mechanism, the less we have to do with it the better. Certainly, we must resist the usual temptation to make a new impulse to cause the arm to travel. The performance should be felt as a simple release of the pent-up energy already contained by the depressed keys, and no more than that.

So we have only the quality of our thinking to consider. Professor Thiberge suggests that the pupil's thought should not be directed downwards into the keyboard. Instead, he should imagine that the keyboard has been raised to a higher level, so that the line of the shoulder and the keyboard is horizontal. Closing the eyes helps; one is often unconsciously influenced by what the visual situation appears to demand. (The sensations of piano playing as consisting of 'up and out' rather than 'down and in' gestures has been remarked on both by Schnabel and Kentner.* To work with a 'mentally raised keyboard' is a splendid psychological device for gaining quick rapport with these sensations of co-ordinated performance.)

The arm is then *allowed* to travel and if the thought is sustained the scale will be accomplished. If the conditions have been perfectly fulfilled, the sensation will be of energy released, not of work being done, and the sound will be louder and more *legato* than

* Kentner, L. *op. cit.* p. 48 and Wolff, K. *The Teaching of Artur Schnabel* pp 24-25 (Faber, 1972)

expected, owing to the absence of those interfering tensions which have led us habitually to associate a certain amount of tone with a much greater effort, and *legato* to be equated with sustaining sounds by means of fingers.

It is unlikely that this ideal state of affairs will be achieved immediately. The processes are really so simple in terms of experience that they are elusive to the majority of people who habitually use themselves in the most complicated and un-co-ordinated manner, whether playing the piano or merely walking down the street. Assuming however that the octaves have been accomplished successfully, Thiberge may invite the pupil to try an ascending scale in octaves, by exactly the same means, using the fingering 3, 4, 3, 4, or perhaps 345, 345:

There should be no difficulty whatsoever for a person of normal sized hands in taking an octave with the thumb and third finger, if he has learned to 'let go' of the contracting muscles, in the hand and forearm. The hand is brought to the keyboard in exactly the same position as before and the third or fourth finger is moved laterally away from the thumb in order to accommodate the octave. We then proceed as before and find that if the conditions are correctly maintained, the outside fingers will crawl over one another without any difficulty. The only difference is a sensation of more sustained energy rather than released energy.

By this time, by dint of numerous repetitions, the student should have acquired sufficient awareness of the requisite conditions to be able to attempt the initial act of key depression for himself. This is a gesture of crucial importance. Even though the hand has been brought to the keyboard in the best possible way, all may be lost unless we are able to equate the action with a general expansion throughout the total posture. There must be no deliberate exertion of the fingers against the keys. Instead the student prepares to meet the upthrust of the key, as already described — and that is all! If one is correctly organised in relation to the keyboard, the fingers have no alternative but to 'expand into the keys'. As we know, the amount of tone is governed by the speed with which the key descends, consequently the amount of tone required will be governed by the speed with which we initiate the gesture. This may range from a comparatively slow gathering of forces for *pianissimo* to a violent spasm *fortissimo*.

Needless to say, loud playing is not to be encouraged in the early stages. The association of loudness with the wrong kind of tension usually takes a very long time to eradicate. Indeed the quality of performance in *fortissimo* is one of the acid tests of co-ordination and a very rapid divider of the 'sheep' from the 'goats' in the world of pianism. A good *fortissimo* is certainly not achieved by practising *fortissimo*, which is just as pointless as any other end-gaining process. All that matters is to acquire the means whereby the end may be achieved.

In addition to the octaves, M. Thiberge gives a few simple exercises, created by exactly the same means which we have already outlined:

In his words: "The transmission of thumb presents no particular difficulty. The thumb is simply placed in position to receive and transmit the pressure like any other finger."

The problem of giving rotary help from the forearm to help the passage of the thumb under the hand, discussed in many text books, is redundant in our system, as this rotation is already present from the beginning. The chief danger to guard against is a tendency to contract in a descending scale or *arpeggio* passage for the right hand, caused by a desire to turn the fingers over the thumb. This can be counteracted by extra attention being given to the lengthening of the arm at this point.

Only one other activity need be mentioned — widespread broken chords:

In the performance of this and similar patterns, the *whole* arm must travel laterally between the two extremes so that the basic relationship of its segments is maintained and continuity of pressure preserved. Particularly important, one must resist the temptation to 'shorten' the arm by pulling backwards on the pivoting finger, which in this example is the second finger. As at all times, the imaginary line of force from the shoulder to the 'raised keyboard' must be preserved.

Once the pupil has grasped the basic principles of posture and touch as applied to these various exercises. Thiberge proceeds directly to the performance of a piece of music, chosen according to the pupil's sight-reading capacity. There is nothing more to be learnt with regard to what is commonly called 'technique'. Provided that the necessary conditions of co-ordination are established and maintained, then the only limiting factor is the pupil's ability to form a mental conception of the work which he wishes to perform. If we can play a work at sight, then we have no need to practise it. In Thiberge's system there is no question of chopping a work up into bits and pieces for the sake of 'practising'.

While the pupil plays, Thiberge is busy checking up on the way the pupil is using himself. The chief problem is to make the pupil aware of any errors which he may commit quite unconsciously during the course of the performance. "Let go of the arm!" he may say, or: "Let go of the knees"! After the passage or movement has been completed, the pupil will be re-adjusted and the passage performed again. The second performance is inevitably an improvement on the first, the third on the second, and so on. Sooner or later, 'it' begins to play; co-ordination has been achieved and previously unimagined refinements of phrasing and colouring suggest themselves. Technique and Art are united at the service of the imagination and the pupil has learnt from the best teacher of all, his own success-ful experience, that fine piano playing is not achieved by overcoming the resistance of the instrument, but by eliminating the resistances within oneself.

Freedom 'from' gives the freedom to 'do'. Ultimately one finds one's own performing style — a personal vocabulary of 'right-doings' related precisely to one's own bodily shape and expressive purposes. In the mean-time one discovers that certain activities which were originally replaced by the single gesture of expansion will re-emerge as spontaneous yet controlled responses to the demands of the music. For instance, under correct conditions some forearm rotation will be found to occur automatically when performing the slow trills which initiate the exercises given on page 71. Furthermore, it will always be the right amount of rotation for the speed and intensity of any given performance. Even from this tiny example we can learn what possession of the 'means whereby' means for the talented performer and learn something of the achievements of the teaching of Raymond Thiberge in this direction.

8 Freedom and Flexibility

"In technique, looseness should come before control, and control before strength". These wise words were penned by Dr. Walter Carroll in the teachers' notes to his album of pieces for beginners: *Scenes at a Farm*, first published in 1912*. They are as true today as they were then, and they apply throughout all stages of development, from the child's first steps to the work of the advanced performer. I prefer to use the term 'freedom' as being more all-embracing than 'looseness', and in earlier chapters I have shown how a gain in co-ordination brings with it a gain in freedom. Unfortunately, some students find their pursuit of freedom limited by residual tensions in the neck and shoulders which prevent them doing full justice to their studies. In such cases, massage is usually helpful. A gentle massage of the back, neck and shoulders also makes an excellent preparation for an Alexander Technique lesson. (I am not so sure, however, about massaging the hands and arms with crude cod liver oil, as advocated by that splendid pianist and composer of light music, the late Billy Mayerl. There are less malodorous products available nowadays.)

It is as true in pianism as it is in politics that the price of freedom is eternal vigilance. To preserve freedom in performance the student must be constantly checking

*   Forsyth Bros., Manchester

that he is maintaining the correct postural conditions, that his arms remain 'long' and that all gestures are made from beneath the relaxed shoulders. This, of course, involves the constant practice of detachment and self-awareness. (This is why the student who genuinely desires to change his manner of playing must submit to the discipline of performing only simple tasks at the keyboard in the first instance, to free him for concentration on these more important matters. Paradoxically, this is the shortest route to the ultimate goal of needing to concentrate only on the music.)

We now come to the question of freedom within the hand, which allows the fingers to move away from, or towards each other, i.e. abduct and adduct, in easy negotiation of the geography of the keyboard, without which fluency is unattainable. The constantly changing figuration of Chopin's *Study in F minor, Op.25 no.2* springs to mind in this context, but lateral flexibility is also required in chords and *arpeggios*, in fact in any texture which goes beyond the simple five-finger position, which means virtually the whole of piano music. It is surprising how many writers dwell at great length on how they believe the fingers ought to move in the vertical plane towards key depression, but take so little interest in their movements in the lateral plane. One does not even have to be a pianist to realise how vertical activity is inflenced by lateral activity; one has only to open the hand out and notice the restriction which this imposes on the vertical movement of the fingers. Conversely, note the difficulty of spreading the fingers when they are flexed. (Let us remember that 'activity' does not necessarily imply movement. When the fingers are spread, for example, they will be maintained in that position by activity in the abducting muscles.)

The inhibition of lateral movement by flexion provides an example of the limitations of the old-fashioned 'bent finger' school of piano playing. A pianist who strictly maintained his fingers bent would find his repertoire restricted to a few simple harpsichord pieces! On the other hand, neither are totally inert 'flat' fingers recommended. There must always be a certain 'readiness' in the finger pads without with perfect control is not possible. Ideally, the fingers should be free and flexible enough to adopt any shape required by the music at any moment.

I should now like to suggest some ways in which lateral freedom may be enhanced in the hand and fingers which will not only give the benefits of improved stretch and flexibility, but improve the quality of touch at the same time, because a gain in lateral freedom means a gain in vertical freedom in the finger, which in turn means again in sensitivity to the resistance of the key. Let us begin by taking the 'matchbox experiment' outlined in Chapter 3 and applying it as follows: place the right hand gently on the keyboard in five-finger position, thumb on C. Then with as much detachment as possible, see the back of the hand widen slowly until the fingers are spread across the interval of a sixth, which is about the limit for normal hands. The next stage is to turn the hand on its axis (still with minimum effort) away from the thumb, until we arrive at the octave of C with the fifth finger. We have now acquired an octave in correct playing position, hand facing outwards, without any stretching of the fingers. Octave should always be taken by moving the hand away from the thumb; moving the thumb away from the hand can easily cause unnecessary tensions, as a moment's experiment will prove. Worst of all is to employ the contracting procedure of grabbing for the octave with thumb and fifth finger simultaneously, which again may easily be verified by experiment.

Having found the octave by the best possible means and depressed it silently, the next task is to move the middle finger over the F sharp key whilst the octave remains depressed. Unless one is fortunate enough to have an unusually large span between the fingers, some resistance to the movement of the finger will be felt, either in the third fingers itself, or in the fourth finger, or both. Readers of this book will understand, of course, that this resistance is not going to be overcome by force. Finger span is never improved by the practice of those dangerous and contracting 'stretching exercises' still perpetuated by some misguided teachers in which the fingers are forced to move violently and vertically whilst being constrained laterally at the same time. Each of us has an alloted span, which may turn out to be wider than suspected as soon as contracting means of performance are abandoned and if the fingers are deployed at the most advantageous angle of incidence.

In the present case, if the hand is allowed to collapse so that it tends to face inwards rather than outwards, the fifth finger lying flat, it will be found that the middle finger will move quite freely to cover the F sharp, without encountering any resistance. Similarly, the fourth finger may be moved over the A key. If the thumb is now released from the task of holding down the C key and allowed to return to its usual position of repose underneath the hand (a full discussion of this point will be found in Chapter 9), the second finger may be moved over E flat and all is now ready for the performance of a descending *arpeggio* on the chord of the diminished seventh.

One important point has yet to be mentioned: a change of hand position automatically involves a re-adjustment of the relationship between the segments of the whole arm. In the process which we have just described, the most obvious feature is that the point of

the elbow moves further away from the body as the
hand turns to face inwards. All segments of the arm
must participate in the constant subtle adjustments of
the hand position required for negotiating the contours
of the keyboard, like the cogs of a well-oiled machine.
The best practice for this will be found in the exercise
on wide-spread broken chords which appears in the
previous chapter and which has value far beyond its
immediately apparent purpose.

The swing of the arm between the extremes of
position demanded by the exercise is exactly that which
is required for all changes of direction in scale and
arpeggio passages. Let us remember that the inward-
looking hand at which we arrived through the
adjustments described above facilitated an *inward-moving
arpeggio*, conversely, if maximum freedom within the
hand is to be preserved during ascending passages in
the right hand, it must be adjusted to look outwards.
Armed with the knowledge now acquired, the reader
should be able to prove this point through his own
research. Apart from octave and other double note
passages, where the hands have to face outwards
irrespective of the direction of travel, the general rule is
that they should 'face the way they are going'.
Furthermore, those readers who were brought up in the
widely held, but mistaken, belief that an inward rotation
of the hand was necessary for the well-being of the
outer fingers and the passage of the thumb, may now
rejoice in their new-found freedom. Enhancing the
striking power of the fingers has no part to play in our
scheme of things, and if the hand is allowed to slope
towards the fifth-finger side in outward moving
passages, the requirement found in some text-books of
"rotation towards the thumb" will be found to be quite
unnecessary. Finally, one more exception to the "face
the way you are going" rule must be mentioned: in

outward travelling chromatic scales in single notes, the hands will tend to remain facing inwards.

To sum up: freedom within the hand requires as much attention as the release of unnecessary contractions throughout the total posture. It is this freedom which allows the hand to change shape and direction with maximum efficiency, although such changes are initiated by gestures of the whole arm. Furthermore, it enables the flowing presentation of the fingers to the keys at always the correct angle of incidence, which is a basic necessity of fine pianism.

9 The Thumb

The thumb deserves a chapter to itself. It is often the most neglected part of our equipment, yet its correct usage is essential to success in our pianistic enterprises. Even when not actively engaged, it exerts its influence. Notice, for example, how freedom in the fingers is diminished if the thumb is extended away from the hand, creating trension in the wrist joint. Unfortunately, the unconsciously extended thumb is often the norm for many students. This results, amongst other things, in the thumb being left behind until the last possible moment in out-going scale and *arpeggio* passages, producing performances which are lumpy at worst and unflowing at best. In a well-trained hand, the tendency for the thumb to travel when the second finger plays is so habitual that it can only be inhibited by willpower.

It is more than likely that the student who leaves his thumb behind is maintaining it in a state of 'connection' to the forearm, one of the most common pianistic faults. Except in special circumstances, the thumb should not be used as an extension of the arm, but should be free to move in its own joint like any other finger. The condition of the thumb may be tested by placing the hand on the keys in the usual five-finger position, swinging the thumb upwards so that it is roughly level with the first flange joints, then letting it fall. (The thumb remains 'long', neither bent nor drawn back.) If the thumb falls freely, its own weight will not suffice to depress the key. If it makes a sound, then remedial work is called for.

For some students, this may take the form of merely ordering the thumb to 'let go'; others may need the thumb to be manipulated by a third party, whilst they concentrate on refusing to 'help' – an Alexander lesson in miniature. (Disciples of Alexander may point out that thumb freedom should be taken care of in the normal course of Alexander technique lessons, but in my experience, this is an area which demands special attention. 'Gripping the thumb' appears to be a habit which is often specifically associated with sitting at the keyboard.)

Once the thumb has been 'disconnected' from the forearm, it should be exercised from its own joint, beginning with vertical movements into the key, where its own muscles will only be sufficient to make a *pianissimo* sound. Anything louder will mean that the forearm muscles are involved, which negates the exercise. Then it can be worked in the horizontal plane, moving under the hand and out again, followed by tone-sounding exercises in different positions in conjunction with the other fingers, as in the time-honoured 'preparatory exercises for scale playing'. Always pianissimo, of course. Another good exercise is to maintain a depressed key with the thumb, then bend and straighten the thumb so that the hand rolls over it and back again.

These exercises are to help the thumb to adapt to the contours of the keyboard by means of its own small muscles. Godowsky advocated playing chromatic scales with the thumb alone, *quasi legato*. Note how in this exercise, the thumb changes shape from 'long' on the black keys to slightly flexed on the white keys – of its own volition, *without any conscious intervention on the part of the performer*, provided it has the freedom to do so.

The normal place of the thumb may be thought of as being inside, rather than outside the hand. In some situations it may even be necessary for the balance of the hand that the thumb is adducted as far as the root of the fourth finger. In certain passages and chords the thumb may substitute for the third or fourth finger, especially if those fingers would be placed in a position of mechanical disadvantage by having to play between the black keys. Busoni said: "The thumb is the centre of the hand", and his pupil Edward Weiss gave me an example of his master's teaching which shows exactly what he meant: Busoni would ask his new pupils to play a rapidly repeated triad of Ab major in the middle register with the left hand. They invariably used the fingerings 531 or 421. Busoni would then ask them to repeat the exercise using the thumb on middle C, so that the fingering was now 512. They were always delighted and astonished by the immediate improvement in ease and control which resulted.

Similarly, I suggest that in figuration such as bar 14 in Bach's *Prelude in C minor* from Book 1 of the "48", the fingering should be 5121, 4121 for the right hand. The use of the thumb on Bb avoids any possible stretching, and the hand should roll easily over the thumb and back again if one is enjoying a co-ordinated performance. Speaking of his early, untutored, experiences at the keyboard, the eminent teacher Peter Feuchtwanger described in an interview, how, when turning round at the top of a C major scale, he found it comfortable to substitute his thumb for his fourth finger, thus the descent began 51321. He said: "My thumb was like the joker in a pack of cards, as it would take the place of any finger. It served as a pivot, and because I used it so much, it never became tense, an affliction which affects so many pianists". (This interview, containing many valuable observations, is printed in *The Massenet Journal* Volume 7*, translated from the original German by Doris Baum and Susette Childeroy Compton under the title: *From Intuition to Reflection.* His lecture: *Bel Canto on a Percussion Instrument?*, reprinted in Volume 6†, is also required reading.)

A word now about placing the thumb on the keyboard. Students often put too much of their thumb on the black keys, causing the problem of over-extension which we have already discussed. There may be occasional cases where this is desirable for emphasis as in the melody notes of Chopin's *C minor Study* op. 25, no. 12, but in those cases the connection with the arm must be conscious and temporary. Release from over-extension usually results in a dramatic improvement in the performance of octave passages. Too much thumb on the keys often causes difficulty with such textures as the repeated chord accompaniment in the right hand of the *Reconnaissance* movement from Schumann's *Carnaval.* The remedy is to ensure that only the tip of the thumb contacts its key. Of course this must not be achieved by over-flexion of the thumb, but by a subtle adjustment of the position of the hand. But there are as many different thumbs as there are pianists, so one cannot lay down hard and fast rules as to how much thumb one should use or what shape it should take. What is important is that the thumb should be free at all times to play its full part in performance and not present any obstacle to the fluidity of one's playing gestures.

* The Massenet Society, London 1988
† ibid 1985

We must be careful to distinguish between extending the thumb in connection with the arm, as in the Chopin study example given above, and lengthening the 'disconnected' thumb, which is so useful for travel about the keyboard. For instance, in the left hand figuration of Chopin's *G major Prelude* op. 28 no. 3, lengthening the thumb on the penultimate semiquaver of each bar automatically despatches the following second finger towards its own key a sixth below, if the performer is making proper use of the upthrust of the piano mechanism. For travel in mid-air, as in skips, the opposite applies. Here, closing the thumb under the hand as it is thrown towards its goal is a positive aid to freedom and accuracy.

This brief survey of 'thumbmanship' would not be complete without mentioning its application in double note passages, where the use of the thumb on two or more keys consecutively is a great aid to speed and *legato*, especially for smaller hands in rapid sixths. The $\frac{3\ 4\ 5}{1\ 1\ 1}$ fingering allows the hand to progress smoothly as opposed to the disturbing zig-zag motion engendered by the customary $\frac{4\ 5\ 4}{1\ 2\ 1}$ fingering. For example, in the second half of the first bar of Chopin's *Study in Db major* op. 25 no. 8, compare the fingering $\frac{3\ 4\ 4}{1\ 1\ 1}\ \frac{5\ 4\ 3}{1\ 1\ 1}$ with $\frac{4\ 5\ 4}{1\ 2\ 1}\ \frac{5\ 4\ 3}{2\ 1\ 4}$ found in most editions. (There are, of course, other fingering possibilities for this passage. I find $\frac{3\ 4\ 4}{1\ 1\ 1}\ \frac{5\ 5\ 3}{2\ 1\ 1}$ best for my hand.) The thumb is the key to liberation from the shackles of those 'legato fingerings' which often negate the every effect they are supposed to produce. The piano is not a *legato* instrument. It is, however, an instrument of infinite suggestion which can be manipulated in many unshackled ways to produce that illusion of *legato* – of fine singing – which is the highest aspiration of the pianist's art. Students often forget that the piano is played with two hands – and at least one pedal. As the 'touch' matures, so should the fingering, and one hopes that today's 'abnormalities', such as the use of the same finger on consecutive keys, may become tomorrow's commonplace choices.

10 Technical Notes on Some Chopin Studies

Chopin was undoubtedly the most progressive teacher of his generation. He was more interested in the performance of music and quality of tone than in the performance of exercises and finger dexterity, and appears to have been the first pianist on record to have condemned the anti-physiological practice of trying to strengthen the fourth and fifth fingers. He was against any unnatural exertions, particularly the violent finger technique practised by the fashionable German school of the time, telling his pupils to 'fondle' the key and not to strike it.

Above all, he wrote the two books of *Studies, op. 10 and op. 25*, which demonstrate so completely his concern with the cultivation of 'touch'. This statement should not cause too many raised eyebrows if the contents of the preceding chapter have been assimilated, although superficially it would appear that many of the studies are concerned more with physical endurance and athleticsm. However, he himself said to a pupil concerning *op. 10 no. 1:* "If you practise this study in the way *I* want, it will widen the spread of your hand and give you *arpeggios* which are like the strokes of· a violinist's bow. But often and alas, instead of teaching these things, it causes them to be unlearnable".

The latter sentence shows his awareness that the demands made by the studies were easily and dangerously liable to mis-interpretation by his contemporaries. It should be noted that Chopin does not talk about stretching the fingers, but about widening the spread of the hand, which is a natural result of the elimination of contracting tendencies, and the analogy of the violinist's bow strokes looks forward to the teaching of Breithaupt on this subject some sixty years later.

On the surface, Chopin's dictum, *Caressez la touche,* appears to offer only a partial solution to the apparently diverse problems of the twenty-four studies. Nevertheless, this is all that is required to play any of them perfectly on the beautifully light actioned Pleyels of Chopin's time, once the right conditions have been established. Anyone fortunate enough to have the opportunity of putting this statement to the test will soon discover that any indulgence in that kind of athleticism which the modern grand piano encourages, not only does violence to the music, but also to the instrument. But even though the modern piano action requires more energy to set it in motion, Chopin's principle remains valid. Whether it manifests itself as a mere caress or a deeper pressure, one touch alone, resulting from the establishment of the correct conditions of co-ordination, is still all that is needed. In the words of Raymond Thiberge:

"It is only because these conditions remain unfulfilled that the student stiffens the wrist when playing octaves, suffers from 'sticking' fingers in the performance of thirds and sixths or is hampered by a 'weak' fourth finger, and so on. The flow of pressure engaging the whole posture presents itself as a totality which realises the activity, 'play', and failures are without exception, the result of superfluous activity. The acquisition of a superior technique requires a perpetual simplification, realised through the choice of the most simple and subtle action, the furthest removed from that kind of struggle with the keyboard which is the negation of all artistic achievement".

Chopin would have surely applauded that last sentence.

The following extracts from Professor Thiberge's notes on the studies,* together with my own comments, provide the student who has mastered our principles with a basis for continued technical development. Only seven studies are mentioned; the same principles apply to all the others, or to any other piano works:

Op. 10 no. 1.

"When confronted by the first study of opus 10, how many students have believed themselves unable to surmount such a degree of difficulty! Unsuccessful attempts naturally deepen their conviction.

However, in the case of failure, it is not the difficulty of the study which is responsible, but the technical procedure employed by the student which renders the execution difficult, and in some cases, impossible.

This study gives the student a marvellous opportunity of determining whether or not he is using correct procedures. In publishing this at the head of his studies, one is tempted to believe that Chopin wished to pose immediately the subtle problem of touch. Unfortunately, pianists are often deceived as to the spirit in which it must be approached.

Formed exclusively of wide-spanning *arpeggios*, this study appears to demand recourse to stretches of the fingers for its execution. But once a pianist knows how to lead his pressure to the extremities of the fingers, he perceives that these *arpeggio* formulae become

* Thiberge, R. *op. cit.* pp. 65-71

possible *as soon as stretches of the fingers are dispensed
with.*

(What happens is that each finger in turn becomes a
pivot for the taking of the next as the arm travels.
There are hardly any abnormally wide intervals between
adjacent fingers throughout the whole piece. When they
do occur, as in bar 30 between the third and second
fingers, they are accommodated by a momentary extra-
lengthening of the fingers in question.)

"A Prix du Conservatoire, as well as Prix de Rome,
dissatisfied with his technique in spite of his large
finger span, came by chance one day to my school in
search of a remedy for his failings. After playing this
study very badly for me, he expressed himself like
this: "Today I have made you sigh, tomorrow I may
play it perfectly well, in either case without knowing
why".

What error did he commit? He allowed his elbow to
'float', maintained a light touch and exclusively concerned himself with not becoming stiff. But he did not
know how to make a sound at the same time!

To embark on the career of pianist without being
able to preserve oneself from this sort of insecurity,
is the unacknowledged fate of far too many otherwise excellent musicians."

Op. 10 No. 2.

"It would appear that the second study, in A minor,
had been conceived in order to seek out any weakness
in the position of the hand. To impose on the hand
simultaneously a design of chromatic scales with the
outer fingers coupled with chords with the inner fingers
is to prescribe a well-determined hand position, in
which a considerable degree of relaxation is demanded
at the same time. Here an inclination towards the
fifth finger side would appear to be indicated, but in

reality, only the reverse adjustment allows this study to be performed successfully. The rotation of the upper arm, point of the elbow outwards, brings about the rotation of the forearm and leans the hand towards the thumb side. In this position, the arm does not turn with the hand, and the hand is articulated freely at the wrist, without any fatigue.

When one knows what the arm can and cannot do, one realises that a backward-tending elbow is going to 'jam' the hand. In fact, obliged to lean towards the thumb in order to play the double notes, the hand finds itself drawn to the fifth finger side by the backward-pulling elbow; the absence of rotation in the upper arm therefore limits the freedom of the hand.

May we repeat that this explanation cannot be understood unless one is acquainted with the possibilities and limitations of the arm?"

(The playing position described here is simply the normal one obtained under expanding conditions. For those who are not blessed with very wide shoulders in relation to the length of their arms (the ideal body-shape for a pianist), a little extra rotation of the upper arm may be desirable. This is one of the easiest concert studies in the repertoire; if it doesn't 'play itself' at first reading, this is salutary proof that the necessary conditions of co-ordination are missing.)

Op. 10 No. 3.

"In the third study, as in the second, the hand assumes a double role: that of melody and accompaniment, but this time the melody must be more expressive and dominate the other textures.

The pianist who does not know how to communicate a pressure to his fingers is going to encounter great difficulty. If he tries to make use of 'finger work' in order to amplify the upper notes, his playing will become dry, colourless and clumsy; the song only begins to rise when the fingers are in firm correspondence with the shoulder. For that, the position outlined for the previous study is indispensable.

With regard to the inflexion of the melodic line, to carry it from one finger to the next demands not only the transmission of the pressure, but a 'lift' on the finger which is being quitted in order to prepare the taking of the next".

(In other words we use each melody finger in turn as a pivot. In this connection, one can give a telling demonstration of the difference between contracting and expanding procedures. Note the contractions engendered in raising the arm by a pull on the supporting finger, compared with the freedom preserved by using a gesture of the upper arm to produce the same result. The visible positions obtained are identical, but the invisible conditions subsisting are completely different.

Of course, it is perfectly possible to play without any undulations of the arm, but this is a musically inhibiting procedure. For the artist, what Magaloff has succintly dubbed "the respiration of the wrist" is an integral part of his quasi-balletic shaping of tone and phrase. Note here the analogy between pianism and dancing with regard to body-usage, perhaps more obviously demonstrated in works such as the *Polonaise in A major* than the work under discussion.)

Op. 10 No. 5.

"The fifth study, entirely on the black keys, is for this reason often estimated to be very difficult. In truth, the demands made by the black keys do not present any special difficulty, save that a faulty adjustment of the arm is going to be accentuated when the hand is engaged in a more forward position on the keyboard. It is then that the pianist feels the necessity

to lean further forward, usually causing the elbow to
fall lower; the wrist then gives the impression of being
raised.

The expression; 'high wrist' is a misnomer. The wrist
has no real personality of its own, since it is only
constituted by the junction of the metacarpus with the
forearm. If the forearm is lowered at the elbow end,
and thus modifies the angle at the other end, this gives
the impression of a high wrist. If on the other hand,
the forearm is maintained at the same level as the
metacarpus, the so-called 'high wrist' disappears.

It is always essential, and particularly on the black
keys, to establish the correct alignment of the segments
of the arm, without which the weight of the arm will
draw the fingers away from the keyboard, instead of
the arm taking the fingers towards the keys".

Op. 25 No. 1.

"The first study of Opus 25, like the first study of
Opus 10, can also be played without stretching the
fingers. The melody, accompanied by wide-spanning
arpeggios, invites pianists to 'float' or throw the hand
about. The upper notes should make a *legato* melody
with its proper inflections, even though they are far
removed from each other. The gesture which unites
them should not consist of swinging the arm, which
would thereby become active, and thrown out of
adjustment. A slight intervention of the body should
carry the hand towards the distant note. The accom-
panying *arpeggios* must also give the impression of a
perfect *legato*. To that end, the elbow must be the
unifying force behind the fingers, and not conspire
to draw them away from the keys."

("Busoni used no swinging movements" — Edward
Weiss. See also the note and example on p. 72.)

Op. 25 No. 2.

"The second study in this set, in F minor, which demands great velocity, will resemble a study of Czerny if the performer is incapable of achieving the necessary crystalline sonority. The pianist who is able to achieve this sonority finds that his arm is resting so lightly in the shoulder that he has the sensation of playing only with the fingers".

(Note that in his remarks on the next study, Thiberge talks of 'liberating' the fingers. They are not forced into activity, but the faster the tempo, the more active or 'free-flowing', in dancing terminology, they become. (See the notes on *staccato* in the following chapter.) If one practises in slow tempo in order to "learn the notes", the only valuable procedure is to use each finger as a pivot for the next as mentioned with regard to Op. 10 No. 3. Truly, touch is all that matters, whether we are dealing with a Chopin Nocturne or a piece of scintillating virtuosity.)

Op. 25 No. 6.

"The study in thirds, in G sharp minor, has certainly been the occasion of much self-deception because it demands a particular perfection of adjustment.

Here it is not a question of liberating the fingers to follow after one another, but of liberating successions of two simultaneous fingers. Velocity, sonority, simultaneity; these results are only achieved by the 'annihilation' of the muscles of the hand, which allows the pressure to arrive at each group of two fingers. No amount of 'hard work' in the conventional sense will give the means of triumph over this study. Only through gentleness, by 'caressing the keys" in the dictum of Chopin, can one master it.

Of course, in caressing the keys, one must know how to lead a pressure to the fingers. The ascending and descending passages demand naturally compensatory gestures of the body, without which stiffness will appear at the joints. (See also the remarks concerning Opus 10 No. 2 with regard to the necessary rotation.)

"The structure of these transcendental pieces forbids all gimmickry, all artificial techniques. It is impossible to triumph over their difficulties at the tempo demanded if one submits them to any kind of assault, for muscular fatigue will soon set in and bring to a halt those who are obstinate enough to persist in that kind of mechanical labour.

It is not surprising that at the time of their appearance, they were criticised as being "finger-breakers". Their essential quality resides in the fact that they *will* break the fingers of those pianists who are ignorant of their errors of adjustment and key-depression.

Any such failures must be considered as a salutary warning to the student. The intelligent study of these pieces proves beyond doubt that technique is not acquired by means of mechanical formulae, but through the true spirit of discovery.

Young pianists should take heart from the following truth: The superiority of the virtuosi stems less from their exceptional faculties than from their discovery of an exceptionally simple means which allows them to use their faculties simply and naturally."

Josef Hofmann aged 10

11 Studying, Repertoire and Performance

Following the principles which have been outlined, we arrive at three main categories of work:

(1) The improvement of co-ordination.

(2) The acquiring of repertoire.

(3) The practising of selected works from one's repertoire with a view to performance.

The nature of the first category has already been defined. The following notes may however be helpful towards further clarification:

It cannot be too strongly emphasised that success in the field of co-ordination is greatly dependent on the mental attitude adopted. We are dealing with experiences so subtle that only the exercise of the utmost awareness will suffice to obtain knowledge of them. The cultivation of awareness demands an attitude of mental detachment so complete that one even ceases to care whether one's goal is achieved or not. The old school-room maxims: "Concentrate!" and "Try hard!" must be banished from our vocabulary, as they have no relevance to the growth of co-ordination, and in fact represent an impedimentary 'end-gaining' attitude of mind which encourages contracting tendencies, as we explained earlier in connection with our 'matchbox' experiment. Misapplied concentration actually diminishes awareness, as in the common case of the student

who becomes so intent on his operations at the keyboard that he fails to hear the sound that he is making.

The attitude must be: "Let us hear and feel what
happens". If the desired result is not achieved, then
the necessary conditions have not been established
and one must retrace one's steps. If the desired result
is achieved, then the extent to which one learns from
this fortunate experience will depend upon one's awareness at the time. Although this attitude to work implies
that one 'does' very little in the accepted sense, the
student must not be surprised to experience the rapid
onset of fatigue in the early stages of growth, coupled
with numerous aches and pains, as muscles which have
previously lain dormant begin to groan and grumble
their way into activity. However, he may take conso-
lation from the knowledge that in our manner of
working he will never suffer from cramps, neuritis and
other symptoms of mal-functioning which have been
known to occur amongst pianists.

The very simplicity of this technical approach sometimes causes it to be regarded with suspicion by the
uninitiated. I have already given examples of its application to the widely differing textures of some Chopin
studies. Here is another example, taken at random.

On the first page of his *Klavierübung*, Busoni presents
us with this co-ordination test:

The required fingering makes execution difficult if not impossible for many people to whom the scale of C major is 'child's play' using the normal fingering.

One could take the exercise to pieces, work at the crossing of the other fingers over the fifth, the passage of the thumb under the fifth finger, practise in different rhythms, and so on, but none of these activities would cause any improvement in the general level of co-ordination. It is because the general level of co-ordination is unsatisfactory that Busoni's fingering appears to be 'difficult', although the level may be superficially satisfactory for the performance of a normally-fingered scale. When the student's co-ordination improves with regard to the performance of the normally-fingered scale, he discovers that the conditions required for its execution and for Busoni's exercise are identical, and the difficulty disappears.

With regard to fingering in general, the higher the level of co-ordination, the less important it becomes, in one sense. Take this extract from the first waltz of Schumann's *Papillons*, for example:

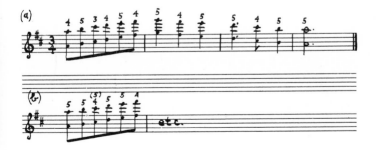

One should be able to produce the same *dolce legato* effect which the music requires, using either fingering. Of course, (a) is better for the travel of the arm, but (b) may be necessary for small hands. From our point of view, if a student lacks the necessary co-ordination to play (a) or (b) with the necessary fluency, he should postpone the addition of such a work to his repertoire. In another sense, fingering is all-important because it reflects — in inexperienced hands, often mars — the subtle adaptive adjustments of the arm which have to be made continuously in most works in order to maintain co-ordination, as well as the artistic intentions of the performer. But any exploration of the numerous 'tricks of the trade' used by advanced performers is unfortunately beyond the scope of this volume. Here, I can only point out that artistic necessity should be the final arbiter of fingering and that the pianist who is forced to choose fingerings on the grounds of 'playability' only is operating on a very low level of co-ordination.

Students are sometimes puzzled by the question of *staccato* playing. Although they see the relevance of the concepts of 'flow' and 'pressure' to *legato* execution, they fail to see how these apply when the notes are detached. There is no difference in the means of performance, however, and nowhere in the whole literature of piano teaching is the confusion between 'ends' and 'means whereby' so completely demonstrated as by the division of piano playing into *'staccato'* and *'legato'* touches. Under the right conditions whether the end-product is *staccato* or *legato* depends on whether one *thinks* one way or the other, and that is all. Anyone who can play the *legato* octaves correctly as outlined in Chapter 5, can automatically play them *staccato* if he chooses to do so. Furthermore, he will discover that in fast tempo, even if he thinks *legato*, the result is inevitably *staccato* and that to all appearances, he is "shaking the octaves out of his sleeve" as Liszt was supposed to do.

The fast octaves become *staccato* because we need to surrender immediately to the upthrust of keys in order to gain velocity. In *legato* playing, the timing of this surrender is deliberately delayed. In the language of dancing, the *legato* octaves represent a 'bound flow' of gesture to which we apply a certain amount of 'tension guidance' and the *staccato* ones represent a 'free flow' in which this guidance is removed. But the flow remains, nevertheless. One should also note that in *staccato* single-finger passages, the touch is identical to that used for *staccato* octaves. The so-called 'finger-staccato' touch described by many writers is not only a contracting procedure — it is manifestly inefficient in comparison with the 'arm-vibration' touch at which we have arrived.

To sum up: many explanations have been proffered as to what Liszt actually did when he "shook his octaves out of his sleeve". The simple truth is that it was the inevitable and natural result of the high degree of co-ordination which that highly co-ordinated man enjoyed with his instrument.

REPERTOIRE

I have suggested previously that the student's repertoire should be confined to works which are within his means at the time. This is not such a limiting prospect as it sounds. The literature of the piano is so vast, that at any stage of progress, copious and valuable additions to one's repertoire may be made — *providing one has the necessary sight-reading ability*. Technique and sight-reading should go hand in hand, so that the student chooses his performing repertoire from amongst a large number of works which he knows he can play — because

he has already played them! Ask any experienced
artist how he learns his repertoire and you will always
get the same reply: "I don't have to — I already know
it."

We should not expect much from a performance by
an actor who had to spell out his lines word for word
before he could begin to learn them. Yet a similar
situation is often accepted in the study of music. I
should like to see abolished completely the time-
wasting and psychologically dangerous attitude fostered
by many conservatoires in which the student's piano
lessons are based on the study of a handful of works
which are beyond his immediate means. Hundreds of
hours may be consumed in the struggle for mastery over
a single work, the net result being a performance which
is dismissed by the critics as nothing more than "a
lesson well-learnt". And what else can one expect under
such conditions?

Of course, by 'sight-reading' I do not mean the ability
to give a rough sketch of the music under pressure,
valuable asset though this is to any musician; I mean
the ability to give a co-ordinated reading, with all aspects
of the work under the control of eye and ear. The reading does not have to be up to speed, but must be rapid
enough to maintain the flow and grasp the broad out-
lines of the work and its details of phraseology. The
commonly held belief that a good sight-reader is a poor
memoriser, and *vice versa*, is only applicable when
sight-reading is considered in terms of making a rough
sketch, and not, as I envisage here the making of a
detailed engraving. Furthermore, engraving a work on
the sensitised plate of the sub-conscious is the fundamental act of memorising. The performer's repertoire
may be likened to a collection of such engravings,
amongst which he browses, choosing those which he
will work over and polish up for public showing.

Without exception, all the great virtuosi are first-class sight-readers, and their huge repertoires stem from the fact that for them, the act of reading and the act of memorising are virtually the same. Moreover, at the highest level of co-ordination the physical presence of the piano becomes unnecessary; the mere sight of the music is sufficient to engrave the work on the aural imagination and in the nervous system at the same time. But at any level, the formation of our conception of a work can be expedited by purely mental rehearsal. Not only does this give us the opportunity of exercising our imagination towards an ideal interpretation, but also of discovering the 'blind spots' where our original image was not correctly engraved. In fact, all lapses, whether of technique or memory, stem from one fundamental cause: a lack of clarity in the formulation of the original conception.

(It is also important that when one plays, one 'thinks the music' just as one is forced to do when rehearsing mentally. Ideally, all one's scores should be learned away from the piano at the very outset, as many artists and teachers advocate, but in my view, this places an unjustifiable limitation on the repertoire of the average student).

The poor sight-reader may ask: "How may I ever reach the stage of being able to assimilate major works by this means?" The answer is: "By working in the way which has already been outlined". The growth of co-ordination brings rewards not only in the isolated sphere of physical activity, but in the co-ordination of hand and eye at the same time. Awareness and experience will do the rest, and no opportunity should be lost of gaining experience in as many branches of musicianship as possible, from choral singing to improvisation, from duet playing to composition. In this connection there is no finer way of gaining platform experience than appearing as an accompanist or ensemble player. Platform nerves are more quickly overcome, as one gets used to the water without having to swim alone, and if one is in the company of more experienced performers, invaluable lessons may be learnt which can be learned in no other situation.

INTERPRETATION AND PERFORMANCE

As mind and body go hand in hand, so do art and technique. In interpretations, therefore, as in other fields, we are governed by the twin factors of awareness and experience. Our conception of a work may be formulated by historical research, analysis, contemplation, playing it, hearing others play it, or any other means, but we can never discover any more about it than we become aware of. Furthermore, as our co-ordination grows, so must our powers of interpretation; over and above our pre-conception of how a work should sound, new subtleties will continually present themselves as the sensitivity of technical response improves. We develop our interpretative powers, not by doing things to the music, such as "putting in the expression", but by letting it do things to us.

This brings us directly to the question of performance, since discussion of purely aesthetic matters of interpretation lies outside the scope of this book. Performance and interpretation are synonymous for all practical purposes, because the way a work sounds in performance *is* our interpretation of that work, whether we like it or not.

In all great performances the element of spontaneity is present. No matter what labours the artist goes to in private to form his ideal conception, he creates his public performance out of the reality of the moment, which is a combined auditory and sensory experience to which his own state of co-ordination, the nature of the instrument, the acoustics of the hall and even the atmosphere of the occasion all contribute. For the mature artist, a performance represents one more voyage of musical discovery, which he views with the detachment of one who is more accustomed to travelling hopefully than attempting to arrive.

For many of us, unfortunately, emotional involvement tarnishes the bright halo of art, and anxiety rocks the boat and turns our voyage of discovery into a scramble for the shore.

Of course, the mature artist travels hopefully because he has already 'arrived', and his degree of detachment is not to be expected from the young artist who is still struggling to achieve recognition. Nevertheless, detachment is the answer to most of the problems of performance, as it implies the absence of emotional involvement, which causes both artistic distortion and unnecessary anxiety.

Detachment stems from 'self-possession'; involvement stems from 'end-possession'. To reap the harvest of maturity one must cease to be 'end-possessed' in order to become 'self-possessed', not obsessed with the struggle for success on the concert platform, but by the desire to become the kind of person to whom successful performances happen. This brings us back to the fundamental question of talent, for the person to whom successful performances happen is, of course, the talented performer.

The successful experiences obtained by the talented performer in the course of his work, from his first acquisition of the scale of Eb major to his hundredth performance of the *Emperor Concerto*, may be traced back to the way he uses himself in order to perform.

Intuitively, if not consciously, he knows that he can

rely upon his co-ordination to guide him on his voyages of discovery. In other words, his self-possession stems from his possession of the 'means whereby'.

At the opposite pole we find the 'end-gainer', who lacks self-possession because he is 'end-possessed'. His mental attachment to the objects of his desire interferes with the means whereby they may be achieved, so that he can only equate success with expenditure of effort. Because he lives by 'works' rather than 'faith', he becomes afraid that he may not have 'done enough' to his programme, either by way of technique or memorising, before venturing on a performance. On the platform, his end-gaining takes the form of attempting to 'make an impression', with the result that he exaggerates, distorts and thereby destroys the interpretations on which he may have spent weeks or months of preparation.

The 'end-gainer' does not necessarily lack innate ability. Talented pianists may be born, but 'end-gainers' are made — by pressures of upbringing, environment and training which only the super-talented may be able to withstand, and to which even they occasionally succumb. Although it is not possible to create talent where the propensity does not exist, the achievements of Raymond Thiberge and Matthias Alexander have at least made it possible for every individual to enter into possession of his rightful inheritance and to release the pent-up stream of talent, allowing it to flow in its natural course. I claim no more for the way of working which I have outlined in these pages, than that it restores hope to the underservingly frustrated, and renders justice to merit. For those who are genuinely called to serve music in any capacity, this is surely enough.

F Matthias Alexander (© S.T.A.T. 1993)

Biographical Notes

F. Matthias Alexander was born in Tasmania and died in London in 1955. He was a self-taught violinist and amateur actor who at the age of twenty-one, after a series of nondescript jobs, embarked on a successful career as a reciter of monologues, and later as teacher, which brought him the directorship of the Sydney Dramatic and Operatic Conservatorium in 1990.

By this time he had already developed his technique for acquiring an improved use of the self, based on the discoveries he had made when analysing the causes of his own hoarseness and loss of voice which had troubled him at the outset of his career and which the usual prescriptions had failed to remedy. He moved to London in 1904, where he set up practice as a teacher of the technique and published his first book: *Man's Supreme Inheritance* in 1910. In 1924, a private school was established at Penhill in Kent for the education of children according to Alexander's principles and in 1930 he established his first training course for the teaching of his method at 16 Ashley Place, Kensington. The war years saw Alexander teaching in the U.S.A., where he had already spent half his time teaching between 1914 and 1924, but he returned to London in 1943 and re-established his teachers' course in 1945. In 1948, the Society of Teachers of the Alexander Technique was founded, which now carries on his work from London House, Fulham, London S.W.10 and publishes the quarterly *Alexander Journal*.

Alexander's books: *Man's Supreme Inheritance, Constructive Conscious Control of the Individual, The Use of the Self,* and *The Universal Constant in Living* are unfortunately now out of print.

Raymond Thiberge was born at Le Mans in 1880 and died in Paris in 1968. Partially-sighted at birth, he became totally blind at the age of nine and received all his musical and general education in the *Institution Nationale des Jeunes Aveugles*. He became a church organist and piano teacher in Chatillon-sur-Seine in 1903. His researches began in 1906 when he went to Germany to consult some of the leading piano teachers of the day, including Elisabeth Caland and Rudolph Breithaupt. In addition to his research into physical co-ordination outlined in Chapter 4, he also studied problems of mental usage with regard to sight-reading and aural training, the first fruit of which was a primitive teaching machine, his *"Auto-Professeur"* of 1912.

Thiberge moved to Paris in 1914 and during the next decade published a piano tutor, several volumes of sight-reading and technical material and a solfège method, all based on 'programmed learning' principles. In 1921 he joined the staff of the *École Normale de Musique* and became its first *Professeur de Pédagogie* in 1925.

In 1931, Thiberge resigned to found his own *Institut Pédagogique* in the rue du Dôme. This became one of the first music schools in Western Europe, where children received general education in the mornings and musical education in the afternoons. By this time Thiberge had realised the value of his teaching principles in general education, which was to become his main concern for the remainder of his life. In 1934 he produced two

films, one on piano teaching, the other on the "formation of thought in younger children" in which he anti-
cipated some of the findings of Piaget over thirty years
later. He devised a correspondence course for parents
in this field and published a French grammar course in
nine volumes, a conjugation and analysis course in six
volumes and an arithmetic course in nine volumes
and summed up his ideas in *Pour ceux qui veulent
mieux apprendre* which appeared in 1939 with a preface
by André Maurois.

The Second World War curtailed the activities of the
Institut, which had featured many public seminars and
performances, including concertos played by children
aged between 8 and 12, but Thiberge organised one
more congress at the *Salle Gaveau* in 1957 devoted to
the theme of the simplification of music studies. He was
made a *Chevalier* of the *Légion d'Honneur* in the same
year and began a campaign for the establishment of a
"laboratory for research into mental and physical
usage", but despite the support of many eminent
people, there was no response from the government.
He continued to teach and campaign vigorously up
to the time of his death at the age of 88, creating a
remedial course in basic concepts for older children
and, between 1966 and 1968, a formation course for
infants as well as writing polemical articles on the
problems of 'backward' children. In 1967, he published
*Une Nécessaire Révolution Pédagogique dans l'Enseign-
ment Musical*, which summarised his thinking on the
teaching of music and piano playing. At the same time
he prepared a similar survey of his work in intellectual
education, which is still in manuscript. Professor
Thiberge's work in this latter field is continued by his
step-daughter, Mlle. Divert-Thiberge at 3 rue du Dôme,
Paris 16, to whom I am indebted for much help in the
preparation of these notes.

Bibliography

Alexander, F.M. *The Use of the Self* (London: Methuen 1932)

Bacon, E. *Notes on the Piano* (Washington: Syracuse University Press 1963)

Banowetz, J. *The Pianist's Guide to Pedaling* (Indiana University Press 1985)

Barlow, W. *The Alexander Principle* (London: Gollancz 1973)

Bonpensiere, L. *New Pathways to Piano Technique* (New York: The Philosophical Library 1953)

Eigeldinger, J-J. *Chopin, Pianist and Teacher* (Cambridge, England: Cambridge University Press 1986)

Fleischmann, T. *Aspects of the Liszt Tradition* (Cork: Adare Press 1986)

Gallwey, W.T. *The Inner Game of Tennis* (London: Jonathan Cape 1975)

Grindea, C. (ed.) *Tensions in the Performance of Music* (London: Kahn and Averill 1978)

Kentner, L. *Piano* (London: Kahn and Averill 1991)

Kochevitski G. *The Art of Piano Playing* (Evanston, Illinois: Summy-Birchard 1967)

Lhevinne, J. *Basic Principles in Piano Playing* (New York: Dover 1972)

Neuhaus, H. *The Art of Piano Playing* (London: Kahn and Averill 1993)

Roës, P. *Music, the Mystery and the Reality* (Chevy Chase, Maryland: E and M Publishing 1978)

Taylor, H.(ed.) *Kentner — A Symposium* (London: Kahn and Averill 1987)

Thiberge, R. *Une Nécessaire Révolution Pédagogique dans L'Enseignement Musical* (Paris, Institut Pedagogique 1967)

Todd, M.E. *The Thinking Body* (New York: Dance Horizons 1968)

Winearls, J. *Modern Dance* (London: A and C Black 1958)

Wolff, K. *The Teaching of Artur Schnabel* (London: Faber 1972)